SIGNIFICANT 72

SIGNIFICANT 72

UNLEASHING THE POWER OF RELATIONSHIPS IN TODAY'S SCHOOLS

Greg Wolcott

POWERFUL • AFFORDABLE • SUSTAINABLE

SIGNIFICANT 72

UNLEASHING THE POWER OF RELATIONSHIPS IN TODAY'S SCHOOLS

Published by FIRST Educational Resources, LLC
Oshkosh, Wisconsin

www.firsteducation-us.com

Cover by:
Ketan Niruke

Printed in the United States of America
(Steinert Printing Company, Oshkosh, Wisconsin)

ISBN: 978-0-578-45562-4

Acknowledgements

Writing this book has been one of the most challenging experiences of my life, and it wouldn't have been possible without the love and support of so many. I have to start by thanking my incredible wife and kids. Lynn, you allow me to live my passion and purpose daily and for that as well as your patience throughout this process, a HUGE THANKS! Maddie, I couldn't have written this book without your insight into what it is like to be a student in today's world. Your constant encouragement and support mean the world to me. Your daily hugs along the way helped, too. Jack, thank you for sacrificing "dad time" and fishing so I could try to make the world better for other people's children. I know these last couple of months haven't been easy. I appreciate your love and understanding.

Mom, Dad, Brad, Bill, and Andy, thank you for being the best teachers a guy could ever have. Your love and guidance over the years has helped me to be a better man, husband, father, and educator.

To my amazing colleagues in Woodridge School District 68, thank you for always pushing me to be a better educator and leader. Your dedication and commitment to children inspires me and empowers me daily.

To Tammy, Garth, and the FIRST Educational Resources family, thank you for believing in me and allowing me the opportunity to work on your incredible team. I hope this book moves FIRST, the leading educational professional development company in North America, one step closer to ensuring high levels of learning for ALL students.

Tom Hierck, not only am I honored to have you write the foreword for this book, I can't thank you enough for your reassurance and encouragement throughout this process. Your belief in my ability to write this book by myself helped me to overcome the self-doubts that crept in along the way. Without your push, I would have given up after Chapter 1. You set the bar high with your vision for this book and challenged me to reach that goal. Thank you for believing in me and helping me spread this message

Special thanks to my former colleagues and students at both the elementary, secondary and graduate level. I have been positively impacted by each and every one of you more than you know. Your stories and struggles inspire me daily.

Finally, thanks to the hundreds of educators who have implemented Significant 72 in their classrooms and shared their success stories with me. Your motivation and enthusiasm for relationship-building served as inspiration throughout this journey.

ABOUT THE AUTHOR

Greg Wolcott currently serves as the Assistant Superintendent for Teaching and Learning at Woodridge School District 68 in Woodridge, Illinois, a suburb 30 miles west of Chicago. As an educator in the Chicagoland area for over 20 years, Greg is passionate about developing opportunities for all students to succeed as well as finding ways for all teachers and staff members to utilize their strengths to maximize the learning of each and every child whom they interact with on a daily basis. Greg consults throughout the United States on a variety of subjects including adult learning, developing innovative practices in the classroom to engage all learners, formative assessment to drive instruction, response to instruction/intervention, and data usage for school improvement.

Dedication

To all the Maddies, Jacks, Sammies, Seannies, Caitlins, Bradys and Emilys of the world, may your teachers be courageous, never give up on you, push you to greatness, allow you the opportunity to make mistakes and struggle, recognize and respect your differences, and love you throughout your learning journey.

Foreword

"People won't care how much you know until they know how much you care."

I remember seeing this quote hanging in the school counselor's office as I began my teaching career and thinking it was just another one of those "feel-good" messages designed to boost a student's self-esteem after they were sent out of class for some quality time with the counselor. Little did I know back then, how the intent of this quote would shape, and continues to shape, my career as an educator. How I wish I had the book you are now holding in your hands, crafted by my friend and colleague Greg Wolcott.

Greg's belief in the efficacy and power of relationships leaps off the pages. He pulls no punches and unequivocally states, "Relationship building is a mindset." But he doesn't leave his colleagues hanging, nor does he devote the pages of this text to pithy meanderings. He provides the solid research to back up his claims and a myriad of tools that every educator can start to use even before they get to the final challenge he issues.

Greg is one of the most amazing educators I have met in regards to his ability to create acronyms. This began as a personal survival skill as he dealt with being a dyslexic learner and has blossomed into a skill that allows all of us to benefit by easily remembering key concepts that he shares (check out the CAP matrix, PRESS, and STORY for examples). In fact, the main chapters of the book are framed around the word COURAGE. This is both easy to remember and a critical need for all educators to demonstrate as they build quality relationships.

Building a quality relationship is, at its core, about creating the positive learning environment that allows every student to experience success, regardless of his or her starting point. We have no control over where a student has been, but absolute capacity to influence where they are going. This is regardless of the student's current status, approach to learning, baggage, or disposition. As Wolcott suggests, "The greater the challenge a teacher places on a student, the greater the importance of the relationships between the two."

This book provides both the challenge and the solution. It will be best used by teams committed to making a difference for all students, who possess the courage to sacrifice short term, temporary gains for long term, sustainable success.

Every teacher, every school, every district can experience this success by taking the time to build positive relationships between all members of the school community. As for the quote at the beginning of this foreword, Wolcott brings clarity to that with the final challenge he issues to his colleagues:

"What can I do today to make sure the time students spend in my classroom is the best part of their day?"

I know this about relationships – if you take the time to build them, all students will learn. I am confident that reading this book will serve as a reminder of the primary reason you became an educator – to make a difference in the lives of ALL students. The impact we have on all students is evident every day. Read on and reconnect with the educator you were destined to be.

Tom Hierck
Educational Consultant and Author
Husband, Father, Grandpa, Colleague, Friend and
Relentless Supporter of High Levels of
Learning for ALL Students

TABLE OF CONTENTS

Chapter 3: Obsess Over the Press......*(29)*

Chapter 4: Unleash Clarity......*(39)*

Chapter 5: Raise the Relevancy......*(53)*

Chapter 6: Accelerate Achievement......*(65)*

Chapter 7: Guarantee Support......*(75)*

Chapter 8: Erase Conflict......*(87)*

INTRODUCTION

Joey was a smart little guy, but like many first graders on the first day of school, he found the full-day experience a little more than he bargained for. Late morning, while struggling to stay focused on learning, Joey abruptly got up and walked out of the classroom. Shocked, his teacher quickly chased after him. By the time she got through the doorway and turned down the hallway she saw Joey, backpack in hand, ready to exit the building.

"Joey," she said, "Where are you going?"

"Home," he replied calmly.

Trying to hold back a smile based on the innocence of his comment, she said, "I'm sorry, honey. But you are staying here."

"But everyone else is going home," he insisted, pointing to all of the kindergarten students getting on the morning bus to leave for the day.

She grabbed Joey's chubby little fingers, looked him in the eye, and said, "You are in first grade this year. You are coming back to class with me. You get to stay here all day." Joey, without a moment of hesitation, looked up at her with his innocent little brown eyes and said, "Who in the hell signed me up for this?" Obviously, school was turning out to be more than he had bargained for.

I don't know about you, but the last decade of education in America has left me on more than one occasion questioning, "Who in the hell signed me up for this?"

New standards, new curriculum, new teaching practices, new assessments, new more rigorous this, and research-based that...while being evaluated on the growth of students who are not yet prepared to meet all this "new." To paraphrase Joshua Medcalf (2015), "The scorecard that society judges us by is tragically flawed and pursuing it is leaving us feeling completely unfulfilled." Teacher burnout and stress levels are at near-record highs across the globe as this "new" era in education has caused many to question their own competence, perceiving that all of their autonomy has been stripped away, and feeling like they no longer belong in the profession.

Instead of living our district mission statements and focusing on the development of the whole child, all too many in our profession have become "number chasers."

Our obsession with "results" has emotionally overwhelmed educators. Unfortunately, the natural reaction of our body's limbic system in times of stress like this is to search for what looks right—not necessarily what is right. Enter the "something shiny" syndrome: the pursuit of the next new thing in the hopes that it will be the elusive silver bullet that will magically allow 100 percent of students to meet or exceed state standards. We are compelled to embrace new ideas and quick fixes, without thoroughly thinking them through. Unfortunately, we are looking in the wrong place. The answer to student success won't be found in a box, be pinned on a Pinterest page, or instantly appear on the Teachers Pay Teachers website. The answer to success is standing right in front of us…looking up at us each day with hopeful eyes.

Insert Significant 72

In his groundbreaking book, *Visible Learning: A Synthesis of Over 800 Meta-Analyses Relating to Achievement* (2009), Professor John Hattie set out to identify which strategies and innovations have the greatest impact on student achievement in schools. In this research, a compilation of over 15 years of work, Hattie synthesized findings from over 50,000 educational research studies on 236 million school-aged students. Hattie grouped these interventions into six categories: contribution from student, from the home, from the school, from the teacher, from the curriculum, and from specific teaching approaches. Next, he ranked these from largest effect to smallest effect, learning that 95% of every educational intervention put in place works. Therefore, the question for investigation wasn't what works, but what works best. Not surprising, the largest effects were found in improvements directly connected to the interaction between teachers and students. In a typical year of instruction, Hattie suggested that a student grows .40 of a standard deviation, equating to 12 months of growth. Among the top 10 interventions listed in his original findings was teacher-student relationships. Teacher-student relationships have an effect size of .72, yielding almost 2 years expected of growth over 1 year. This should be considered a significant impact by any definition!

As Hattie's (2009) research showed, positive teacher-student relationships are one of the most powerful keys to success in any classroom. In 2012, Robert Pianta—one of the foremost researchers on the topic of teacher-student relationships—and his colleagues stated, "Positive relationships with adults are perhaps the single most important ingredient in promoting positive student development" (p. 381).

These relationships lead to greater academic outcomes, including marked improvement in the areas of reading, math, student participation, student motivation, critical thinking ability, and engagement (Hughes et al., 2008; Martin & Dowson, 2009; Roorda, Koomen, Spilt, & Oort, 2011). Social-emotional outcomes such as an enhanced ability to adjust to school, better social skills, increased self-efficacy, and more efficient problem-solving have also been shown (Buyse, Verschueren, Verachtert, & Van Damme, 2009).

Further, Cornelius-White (2007) attributed stronger relationships in the classroom to increases in student attendance, as well as decreases in disruptive behavior and dropout rate.

Based upon a preponderance of research evidence, it is hard to disagree that high-quality relationships in the classroom are the foundation for success. When diving deeper into the research on the topic, however, one begins to uncover some of the intricacies often overlooked when considering the topic of relationships. But first, let's make sure we are all on the same page. What is the definition of a high-quality relationship? Positive teacher-student relationships are those marked by high levels of closeness and low levels of conflict. Pretty simple? Not so fast. For maximum effectiveness, we need to know when, with whom, and to what degree each affects the learner relationship. Knowing these nuances is what separates the good from the great.

Effects of Teacher-Student Relationships by Age

Because younger children spend the majority of their school day with one teacher, it is easier for them to connect. The inherent need for security is met easily in the classroom. A bond and closeness develop more easily in this environment. Thus, the effects of high levels of closeness, although important, aren't as dramatic at the younger age. The real influence is the degree of conflict noted in the relationship.

Younger children are impacted greatly by negative relationships in the classroom. These undesirable relationships affect younger children more and stay with them longer. Younger children often find it very difficult to get over incidents of conflict. Hamre and Pianta (2005) found that conflict not only damages relationships, but causes heightened levels of stress and insecurity within children. Teachers at the elementary grades need to be more cognizant when relationships are on the rocks, and quickly move to repair these fractures, because the ramifications have lasting effects.

Because they are more mature and their brains are more developed, older students can get over, or brush off, conflict a little more easily. Disturbances affect them but can quickly be repaired. Unfortunately, the quality of relationships decreases as kids grow older (McGrath & VanBergen, 2015).

Older students are inspired by the guidance they received during the middle and high school years. Positive relationships lead to increased engagement and achievement at these ages.

As students transition from elementary to middle school, they go from spending the majority of their day with one teacher to suddenly being asked to bond with a half dozen or more.

This makes it much more difficult for them to know their teachers on a personal level. Middle school students who don't bond with their teachers are much more likely to feel disengaged and alienated than their peers (Murdock, Anderman, & Hodge, 2000).

From a teacher's perspective, working with 200 students or more each day makes it very hard to personally connect with each child. Teachers of older children must be more intentional and work harder to develop relationships with their students. These efforts are worth their weight in gold, however, as students who feel their teachers care and support them through their learning journey are more motivated and work harder (Wentzel, 1997). Unfortunately, too many secondary level teachers end up focusing more effort on their curriculum than on their connections. This focus on the fruit and not the root leads to lower levels of success in all areas.

Based on the information mentioned, it is no surprise that although positive relationships are beneficial to children of all ages, these relationships are particularly beneficial to older students, and overall, "Stronger effects were found in higher grades" (Roorda et al., 2011).

Gender

As I will discuss in Chapter 2, similarities lead to success. Students who have attributes in common with their teachers, achieve at higher levels. Based on the fact that approximately 80 percent of teachers in America are female, it is no surprise that female students report having more secure attachments with their teachers than male students (Sabol & Pianta, 2012). According to Hamre and Pianta (2001), female students also experience less conflict in their relationships. Male teachers also report finding it easier to develop relationships with female students. Because closer relationships lead to more engagement and attention, however, compliance often overshadows learning needs. This makes it crucial for teachers to truly get to know each student's individual needs in order to provide the best possible learning opportunities and ensure that each child can thrive.

Boys, on the other hand, do not typically enjoy the same level of closeness with their teachers. This leads to a lack of motivation to learn and decreased levels of on-task behavior, regardless of the teacher being male or female. More conflict is reported among male students of all ages (Sabol & Pianta, 2012). These findings reinforce the need for teachers to add to their toolbox of strategies to reach students of both sexes.

Race and Ethnicity

Although strong teacher-student relationships impact all students, ethnic and minority students benefit most. Meehan, Hughes, and Cavell (2003) reported that African American and Hispanic children appear to benefit more from close relationships with their teachers than Caucasian students.

Positive teacher-student relationships are of utmost importance to students of color. Lisa Delpit, author of *Multiplication is for White People: Raising Expectations for Other People's Children* (2012), wrote that "Many of our children of color don't learn from a teacher, as much as for a teacher. They don't want to disappoint a teacher who they feel believes in them. They may, especially if they are older, resist the teacher's pushing initially, but they are disappointed if the teacher gives up, stops pushing" (p. 86).

At-Risk Students

The number of students attending school who come from low-income homes or have learning difficulties is increasing across the globe. The challenges that these children face can have huge impact on their ability to learn and succeed in school and in life. At-risk students, however, benefit more from robust relationships with teachers than average students (Roorda et al., 2011). In fact, relationships are a protective factor and act as a buffer against many of the barriers that children in need face throughout their school day (Fosen, 2016; Ladd & Burgess, 2001).

Positive teacher-student relationships serve as a resource for students at-risk of school failure, whereas conflict or disconnection between students and adults may compound the effects of being at-risk (Ladd & Burgess, 2001).

Behavior

One of the greatest sources of conflict in the teacher-student relationship is student behavior. Relationship quality is most notably affected by students' externalizing behaviors such as talking out, non-compliance, gross disrespect, or fighting. Although extremely challenging, these behaviors are usually visible within the walls of the school. Internalizing behaviors such as depression, anxiety, social withdrawal and school avoidance, however, are not easily recognized within the classroom, but these also affect a student's connection with the teacher. Fortunately, positive teacher-student relationships have been proven to help children dealing with both. Close relationships with teachers are associated with improved academic and socioemotional functioning among children with externalizing and internalizing problems (Ladd & Burgess, 2001; Sabol & Pianta, 2012).

Teacher Well-Being

Take a minute and think of a student with whom you had a close relationship. Were you a little more enthusiastic to work with that student than others? When that child succeeded, did you feel like you succeeded? Did you get as much as you gave? I am sure that the answer to all of the above was yes. And it is absolutely no surprise. We all entered the profession because we love kids; unfortunately, due to the demands mentioned early in the chapter, we have at times misplaced that love. We can no longer! Those connections fuel us.

It is no surprise that researchers Spilt, Koomen, and Thijs (2011) noted the positive impacts and intrinsic satisfaction garnered from forming close relationships with students. These connections lead to greater job satisfaction, higher effectiveness, a feeling of competence, and a feeling of purpose. When the relationships and connections are good, we feel better about our abilities. The closer the relationship with students, the more that teachers' self-efficacy beliefs increase (Mashburn et al., 2008). But, when relationships go south, so do our feelings about ourselves. When we fail to take the time to fully develop those relationships and let negative interactions rule the day, we are more prone to burnout and anxiety (Chang, 2009; Spilt et al., 2011).

One Final Fact

What is the single most important school-based predictor of academic growth in the math classroom from eighth to 12th grade? Is it students' prior knowledge? Their interest in math? Their past success in math? Teachers' subject-matter knowledge? Parents' education? No, none of the above!

Gregory and Weinstein (2004) concluded that the single most important school-based predictor of academic growth in the math classroom from eighth to 12th grade was a student's perception of "connectedness" with his or her teachers. One may wonder why "connectedness" is such a key factor on student success in the math classroom. To answer that question, I would ask that we pause and take a look at what happens in the typical math classroom. In most math classrooms, we see lots of challenges—not only challenge in the problems, but in the environment. Students move in and out of their comfort zones and failure is common place. Trial and error in front of the teacher and the peers is the norm, and only the resilient students succeed. It is vital that students in this environment have a teacher who shows interest in them, who makes math relevant in order to motivate them to tackle challenging tasks, celebrates every small success along the way, and offers support and praise for the ongoing effort and perseverance.

BAM! THIS IS WHY RELATIONSHIPS ARE SO IMPORTANT! As Hattie (2012) stated, "The positive teacher-student relationship is thus important not so much because this is worthwhile in itself, but because it helps build the trust to make mistakes, to ask for help, to build confidence to try again, and for students to know they will not look silly when they don't get it the first time" (p. 21). Great teachers leverage the relationships they form to create the conditions for students to not only survive, but thrive!

Yes, there is no doubt that the overall effects of relationship-building are impressive. Relationship development should be an ongoing and intentional part of everything we do in schools. Unfortunately, that is not happening. So we must ask, "Why?"

The Five Whys

Faced with the task of solving a difficult problem, I often turn to the "Five Whys" protocol. This simple technique helps me to quickly get to the bottom of a problem and uncover the root cause. This systematic process begins by simply asking the question "why" five times and answering each question honestly. When applying this technique to the issue at hand with a group of educators one summer, the process went something like this:

1. *Why aren't all teachers taking the time to cultivate relationship-based environments within their classrooms and learning spaces?*
   ➔ *"Because we don't have enough time."*

2. *Why don't we have enough time?*
   ➔ *"Because there is too much content to teach and we can't cover it all as it is. Developing relationships takes time."*

3. *Why do we have to "cover" it all?*
   ➔ *"Because if we don't cover it all, our students won't know what they need to know to be prepared for the standardized tests. Standardized tests determine our evaluations and school ratings."*

4. *Why can't we be successful on academic measures and build relationships at the same time?*
   ➔ *"Because we have never done it that way before.*

5. *Why are we being held back from trying a new approach?*
   ➔ *"Uhh…truth? If we try something different, it may not work out. We might actually have worse results."*

There, we have it…self-doubt! What is holding us back is the fear of the unknown, the lack of confidence within us, and the little voice in our head reminding us of what could go wrong instead of what could go right. Although this is a totally normal thought process, our own insecurities are holding us back from pursuing a better way. It is natural to wonder if you can get similar results to those proven by research. It is common to question if your students will experience greater levels of success than previous groups, and it is expected that you will want to know if you are "doing it right."

As my colleague, Tom Hierck, reminds educators across the globe, the opposite of self-doubt is courage. Courage is exactly what it's going to take to help all of our children meet and exceed the demands of life. Building quality relationships in the classroom isn't easy. This is not something done in a day, a couple days, a week, or even a month. Relationship-building is a mindset.

Teachers must recognize there will be good days and bad. They will need to do the little things day in and day out, over and over again. It won't be easy. It will take courage to make relationship-building in the classroom a higher priority than the curriculum to be taught. When done right, however, it is the most satisfying experience ever, for both you and your students.

Relationship-Building

Significant 72: Unleashing the Power of Relationships in Today's Schools has been written to inspire you to form deep connections with each and every student who enters your learning space. It is my goal to provide a rationale for those who are hesitant to make relationship-building a priority, to reconsider their actions, to remind themselves why they entered the profession in the first place, and to provide them with a courageous alternative to the status quo. At the same time, I want to further empower those who are natural relationship builders with research-informed, evidence-based, teacher-tested, and kid-approved ideas, strategies, and techniques to increase students' social emotional and academic skills by developing stronger teacher-student relationships in the classroom.

Many of the ways in which we view the formation and purpose of relationships in the classroom is based upon faulty models. Despite what we may have experienced as students ourselves, what we were taught in undergrad, and what we have seen in colleagues classrooms, or heard within the walls of the faculty lounge has led us astray. We have to take a new approach.

As I expect everyone reading this book to challenge and push their students out of their comfort zones, I will be doing the same. I will continuously challenge some of your underlying beliefs and push you to reflect upon whether your daily actions align with the intended outcomes that you work so hard to attain. Rethinking how and why you do what and why you do it will be key to your growth and that of your students.

Each chapter will begin with a message from my daughter, Maddie. This message serves as the why for which the chapter is important. At the end of each chapter, I have included a number of questions to help you reflect upon your practice, rethink how and why you teach like you do, and refine the way you interact with children.

In summary, if you are looking for a way to increase your own well-being and improve student motivation, engagement, and achievement, look no further. You have come to the right place.

About this Book

In **Chapter 1**, we start by looking at our most memorable teachers. What did they do that others didn't do to have such impact on our lives? We will then talk about the four types of teachers that are prevalent in today's schools, and determine which one is the one who can actually produce the social, emotional and academic outcomes today's world demands.

As you have picked up already, developing robust teacher-student relationships in the classroom takes courage. In Chapters 2 through 8, I will introduce you to the seven vital teacher behaviors needed to have a significant impact on student success and the important messages each send to students. The first letter of each chapter spells out the word "courage," as a reminder that these actions are not easy, but essential to student success.

Chapter 2: Create Connections. In this chapter, we describe the importance of connecting with the students in your classroom. We discuss ways educators can develop connections as well as kill connections.

Chapter 3: Obsess Over The Press. Here we explore the importance of pressing students academically. Readers will learn about the seven areas in which students must be challenged to excel.

Chapter 4: Unleash Clarity. This chapter deals with making sure we make learning clear to students. Knowing your students well and knowing ourselves well impacts the clarity we provide.

Chapter 5: Raise the Relevancy. Because students learn better when they are interested in the topic, this chapter is devoted to talking about how the teacher-student relationship can be leveraged to enhance student motivation.

Chapter 6: Accelerate Achievement. Ensuring students experience success is critical to increasing their self-efficacy. In this chapter, we dive into ways teachers can help students get on winning streaks in the classroom.

Chapter 7: Guarantee Support. A supportive environment is crucial to student success. In this chapter, we explain the impact that learning in a psychologically safe atmosphere has on student engagement and achievement.

Chapter 8: Erase Conflict. Although no teacher wants to experience conflict with students, it is inevitable. In this chapter we learn ways to better understand student needs and manage the cycle of conflict that sometimes occurs between students and teachers.

In **Chapter 9**, we will wrap things up with a challenge to act. We will explore the impact one caring teacher can have on the life of a child, discussing students who are more at-risk and how we can help them be successful. We will then end by talking about how the two opposite energies so prevalent in the classroom are actually complimentary and must flow together to ensure the success of both teachers and students. Are YOU ready to dive in? I am, so let's do this!

CHAPTER 1

TEACHING TODAY

Maddie's Message:
I know I matter when my teacher creates the conditions for me to learn.

It was 4:00 PM on a cold and dreary Wednesday afternoon. Like thousands of other educators, I was rushing out of school to go to graduate class. Unlike most, I wasn't taking the class, I was teaching the class.

As I entered the classroom, I had empathy for the 22 people sitting in front of me. These incredibly hard-working, talented, and devoted educators were putting their lives on hold to better themselves and the lives of the students. Sure, obtaining their master's or doctoral degree was the end goal, but surviving a 16- to 18-hour day was foremost on everyone's minds.

Transitioning from teaching all day, to quickly getting in a car to drive to graduate class can be a challenge. After a full day with children, immediately immersing oneself into learning about educational research isn't always easy. To relieve some of the tension, I had found a little trick—a way to put a little space between events and ease them into new learning for the night. The trick came in the form of small, squeezable foam toys.

Each night, I would start the discussion by passing a foam toy around as a conversation starter. Along with the prop, I would give students a sentence starter to complete. This sharing became a fun way to get to know each other, create a sense of belonging, and establish the purpose of the evening in a very non-threatening way. The toys and topics included a small squeezable camera to discuss a picture of something great that happened in their own classrooms the week before, a remote-control television clicker to share one thing they would redo if they could "push rewind" on a lesson that hadn't gone as planned, or a flexed arm muscle to share their strengths as an educator.

Not only did their thoughts and words provide an invaluable look into what happens in our classrooms, but the motivation from hearing great educators talk about what makes learning magical for students was inspiring. The success stories they would share, and their evidence of student growth were profound and carry much more weight than those measured by standardized tests. These men and women changed lives. As a research geek, I wanted to learn from them in hopes of replicating the effects.

Instead of living our district mission statements and focusing on the development of the whole child, all too many in our profession have become "number chasers."

For one night's opening activity, it was a foam "Oscar Award" trophy. I would pass the bright gold statuette around and ask students to name a phenomenal teacher they had had when they were younger. Then, I would be asking them to identify what those talented men and women had done to excel and earn this merit of excellence. Responses on this particular evening would be tabulated along with those of over 400 others as part of my own personal seven-year research.

That night's answers held true to form. Like hundreds before them, graduate students remembered, and felt most impacted by, teachers who built strong teacher-student relationships. More specifically, over 90 percent of the "great teachers" that the participants recognized shared two critical characteristics: they exhibited high levels of care and concern toward student social and emotional well-being, and they showed high levels of challenge by insisting on academic growth and excellence. Those recognized for distinction developed an incredible bond with each child and then leveraged that connection to help students achieve at high levels.

A Deeper Dive

I know what you might be thinking, "All teachers exhibit these two behaviors, don't they?" Yes, these two factors are present in every classroom, but it isn't the mere presence of these behaviors that makes a difference; it is the level of each that creates the real impact.

Adapting from Judith Kleinfeld's (1975) seminal study of Alaskan teachers and Diana Baumrind's (1968) work on parenting types, it is possible to group today's teachers into categories based upon the levels of each factor. But first, let's take a closer look at these two components: care and press.

Care

Teachers who care display genuine interest and personal regard for each student. They are attentive to students' needs and create a safe, supportive learning environment. Students who are members of a caring teacher's classroom community feel a sense of closeness to the teacher and feel comfortable approaching the teacher for both academic and emotional support. This environment is one where the teacher not only listens and demonstrates concern for each student, but shows a sensitivity and responsiveness to student feelings.

Care, however, cannot be taken for granted within today's schools. Survey results from the 2016 School Voice Report, developed by the Quaglia Institute for School Voice and Aspirations, showed that slightly more than half of students (53%) reported that their teachers care about them as an individual.

In contrast, only 43% of students reported that their teachers care about their feelings and problems.

Increasing care in the classroom is vitally important to overall student success. Care is not only a strong predictor for increased college aspirations and one's love for continual learning (Ferguson, Phillips, Rowley, & Friedlander, 2015), but it also impacts a student's achievement in the moment. Dweck, Walton, and Cohen (2014) reported that "the perception that teachers care about their students is among the strongest predictors of student performance" (p. 11).

Why does care have such a lasting effect? The answer is simple. Creating a caring environment provides students the psychological safety needed to take risks, bounce back from errors and mistakes, ask for assistance when needed, and overcome failure, while also achieving at high levels.

Academic Press

Academic press is defined here as a child's perception of being challenged academically to master what is being taught. Press is about the rigor and accountability students experience on a daily basis. It requires teachers to ensure students not only know the answers, but know the material well enough that they can explain their thinking and transfer the learning to new and novel situations. Press calls for teachers to push children beyond their comfort zone in order to succeed, not allowing them to give up when difficulty arises.

It is important for educators not to look at academic press as synonymous with having high expectations. As will be discussed later in the book, teacher expectations of students are susceptible to bias and can be unintentionally lowered without conscious thought; therefore, having high expectations isn't enough. Pushing students to persist through struggle in order to develop deep understanding of material, while being held accountable for learning at high levels, is what really impacts one's future advancement.

This feeling of being pressed for understanding is significantly correlated to student success in the classroom. Shouse (1996) found that higher academic press is not only positively correlated to higher levels of academic accomplishment, but is a statistically significant predictor of school achievement. More recently, results of Bill and Melinda Gates Foundation's Measures of Effective Teaching study have shown annual achievement gains on standardized tests are predicted most strongly by aspects of academic press (Ferguson et al., 2015).

The CAP Matrix

The Care/Academic Press (CAP) Matrix is a four-quadrant model developed to learn more about the effects of combining the two key characteristics of great teachers. On the vertical scale, we measure student perceptions of how much a teacher cares, from low to high. Then, on the horizontal scale from low to high, we measure a student's perception of the academic press. This construct illustrates that today's educators fall into four distinct categories. Although there are benefits to each, only one creates the lasting effects needed to prepare students properly for the world ahead.

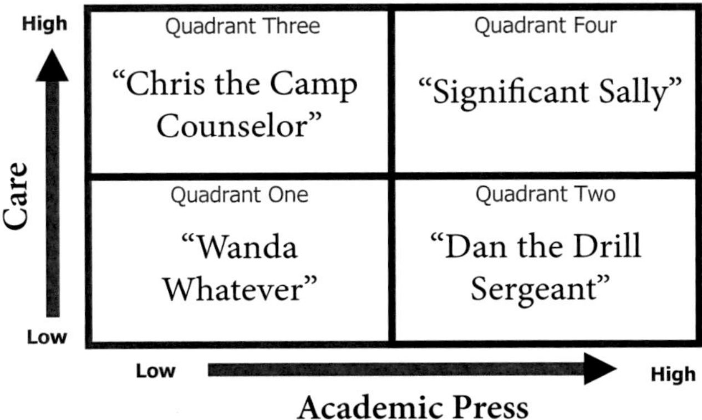

Figure 1. The CAP Matrix.

The Four Teachers: A Closer Look

In the lower left quadrant, quadrant one, we find "Wanda Whatever." Wanda's classroom is characterized by low levels of care and press. Students in Wanda's class don't feel loved or pushed to succeed. Their only concern is surviving the class period, so they can get on with the day. There are no boundaries and little to no discipline in the classroom. Students in Wanda's room have a propensity to misbehave due to boredom and lack of authentic engagement. Students who come into her classroom from solid backgrounds have a chance to succeed based upon the self-regulatory skills they have developed over time. Students who haven't been so fortunate to grow up in an equally supportive environment tend to struggle.

Wanda exhibits the classic "coast" mentality. She has no sense of urgency at all in her teaching, and does not go out of her way to get to know students. She believes that as long as she shows up and teaches what she is supposed to teach, she is doing her job. She is typically cold and unresponsive. She communicates an indifference to most things and never gets involved in any aspects of the school community. At times, she will act very impulsively, causing students anxiety. This environment, although predictable in some respects, sends a message of "I don't care" to students.

In the next quadrant, we have "Dan the Drill Sergeant." Children in Dan's class are painfully aware of rules and consequences.

Hard, fast, and rigid deadlines rule the day. Students are pushed to achieve at high levels and are held accountable for meeting or not meeting the challenges put in place. Many are afraid to take chances, fearing criticism from Dan and embarrassment in front of their peers. Dan's classroom is not an emotionally safe environment. Due to the lack of care students are often left feeling frustrated when struggle lingers often affecting students' self-esteem and negatively impacting their sense of self-efficacy.

Dan is hard working, no-nonsense, and organized. He feels a great sense of responsibility for delivering curriculum. He takes comfort in knowing he is covering the curriculum as told and takes that job seriously. Unfortunately, his compliance-based mentality leads to a focus on teaching rather than on learning. Dan tends to blame a lack of student progress on the students' effort, attitude, and behavior. Internally feeling a lack of competence when students do not succeed, his anxiety is passed down to his students. The result is often displayed in the form of yelling or harsh consequences. All of these factors lead to an environment with little psychological safety, which impacts student trust in Dan and their belief that mistakes are part of the learning process. They choose to stay within their own comfort zones, afraid of looking bad if something goes wrong when they venture out. Dan has no sympathy for students who don't meet the challenges he sets, and they know it.

Achievement gaps widen for students in Dan's classroom. In order to have an excuse when students do not succeed, Dan places ceilings on what some students are capable of achieving. These limits are all too often subject to Dan's internal biases around race, income level, language acquisition and learning differences. Students who have grown up in supportive environments in the past, can survive their time in Dan's classroom. Students who haven't had that luxury, however, suffer greatly.

In the third quadrant we have "Chris the Camp Counselor." Chris' students enjoy being in her classroom. She is fun-loving, incredibly responsive to student needs, yet very lenient of their behaviors. They gravitate toward her "every child gets a trophy" attitude. Students love sharing their stories and personal experiences with her, knowing she will always listen. Unfortunately, this permissive behavior comes at the expense of learning. Because students aren't as challenged academically as they could be, they fail to grow intellectually at the rates of students in classrooms with higher levels of press.

Chris loves being a teacher. She invests heavily into knowing her students and is genetically wired to nurture. She cares deeply about her students and loves being thought of as a friend. She individually sets expectations for each child's learning based upon their circumstances or wants, rather than their needs. This can become problematic, as sympathy often dictates the level of academic challenge a student will face in her classroom. When students experience academic wobble, she often makes learning easier, not allowing them to experience the productive struggle needed to learn skills such as perseverance and grit.

Chris' classroom is highly emotional. Things are either really fun and joyous, or not. This takes a heavy toll on students who have higher social emotional needs. Student academic rigor is often lost in order to ensure emotional comfort. At times, Chris becomes a coddler, protecting students from failure at all costs. This pampering deprives her students of many important social emotional learning lessons. The emotional dependency created doesn't serve as a benefit to enhanced academic learning or lifelong success.

Chris measures her sense of success on the relationships she builds; however, she is keenly aware of the lack of academic press that her students experience. This awareness can be internalized and may lead to burnout and a sense of frustration with herself and her superiors.

Students who come from strong academic backgrounds and who have formed strong work habits from previous experience come through ok in Chris' classroom. Their internal drive for success buffers them from lack of challenge provided by the teacher. Unfortunately, students who do not have solid academic experiences before entering, suffer in the quadrant three classroom. Although many of these students will report they enjoy going to class, that enjoyment does not translate into learning gains. Academically, they do not grow at a rate needed to be successful at the next level. Social skills also do not develop at an appropriate rate.

Anecdotal research based on extensive conversations with colleagues across the country, observation in hundreds of classrooms, and one on one talks with dozens of students, indicates a large number of today's teachers fall within category three, focusing more on students' comfort than competence.

In quadrant four, we find "Significant Sally." Sally is the teacher that my graduate students described as having the greatest impact on their lives. Teachers in this category realize that student success is not an "either-or" proposal. They understand that in order to meet the academic rigor of the 21st century classroom, students need a teacher who cares about them deeply and demonstrates high levels of warmth. Even when in the classroom of an extremely caring teacher, a student needs to be pressed for understanding and held accountable for learning.

Learners in Sally's classroom find the space not only warm and encouraging, but disciplined and structured as well. They know that she may come off as firm at times, while she insists on their success, but they know it comes from a place of care. She consistently sends a message to them that they are important enough to be pushed and places no ceilings on their learning. They know that she believes they are all capable of accomplishing anything, and they will work hard for her to prove it.

Sally bases her success on students' success. If students are successful, then she feels she has done her job.

If, however, children are not successful, she will hold herself responsible for helping them flourish. She believes that all children can and will learn at high levels in her classroom. And, she will do everything within in her control to make that happen. She understands that struggle is the key to learning and ensures students experience that academic wobble when they are in her presence, guiding and supporting them along the way.

Students from all backgrounds, income levels, and ethnic groups benefit from teachers like Significant Sally. Recently, however, researchers have indicated that students of color particularly benefit from teachers who exhibit high levels of trust, care, and communication, as well as set a high bar for student success and press them to meet or exceed those standards (Butler, personal communication, 2017). Further, Butler indicated that students of color do not feel cared for if they are not urged to excel at high levels. And, at the same time, students perceive that a teacher who doesn't set clearly defined standards for them and insists on achievement really doesn't care. Such findings make becoming a quadrant four teacher a must for any teacher working with students of color.

Respectfully Relentless

Dr. Bill Schmidt—a former junior high principal and four-time state champion football coach at Immaculate Conception High School in Elmhurst, Illinois—epitomizes the courageous teacher with his slogan for success. Dr. Schmidt credited his success in the classroom and on the athletic fields to being "respectfully relentless," or constantly challenging students to go farther and reach higher while at the same time loving them up along the way.

Yes, some students will learn despite their teacher. They will learn no matter who their teacher is and what quadrant the teacher falls. However, I firmly believe if we truly want to close achievement gaps and develop students with the knowledge, skills and attitudes to be successful in the 21st century, we must aspire to have a Significant Sally in every classroom. These respectfully relentless teachers, who have the courage to not only exhibit high levels of care but also push students daily to reach for the stars, are our best hope. The remainder of this book explains how you can become such an inspiration.

Reflect/Rethink/Refine

- *Who was your favorite teacher? What makes that person so memorable?*
- *Who was your least favorite teacher? Using the CAP Matrix, which category did that teacher fall in?*
- *Using the CAP Matrix, what quadrant do you fall in as a teacher?*
- *What changes would you need to make to consistently teach like "Significant Sally"?*
- *In what ways can you and your colleagues be more "respectfully relentless" about student learning?*

CREATE CONNECTIONS

CHAPTER 2

Maddie's Message:
I know I matter when my teacher makes me feel safe and special.

We have all seen the viral, heart-warming videos of teachers welcoming students into classrooms across the country. There they are, twenty plus students, all in a line, patiently, yet excitedly, awaiting their daily dose of relationship juice, which comes in the form of personalized handshakes, high fives, and hugs. One can't help but be energized seeing these interactions. These brief exchanges between adult and child are the epitome of connection.

Not only do such welcomes provide students a predictable and consistent start to the day, but they literally alter students' brain chemistry. Supportive connections with trusted others causes the brain to release oxytocin, the love and belonging chemical. Oxytocin, in turn, calms the amygdala, the brain's fear center, and helps students control their emotions. These interactions also reduce the release of cortisol, the stress hormone, by discharging endorphins, serotonin and dopamine. This powerful trio helps students more easily access the frontal areas of the brain, where executive functioning and learning occurs. Simply put, connection is the keystone of every successful classroom.

Brené Brown (2013) defined connection as the "energy that exists between people when they feel seen, heard and valued; when they can give and receive without judgment; and when they derive sustenance and strength from the relationship." The combination of feeling seen, heard and valued lets people know they matter. When we know we matter, we trust those around us, we are open to new ideas, and we are willing to be vulnerable. We feel the emotional safety needed to take chances, move out of our comfort zones, and live in the moment, not worrying that we will fall prey to judgment and critique. Courageous teachers realize that these attributes are needed for student success and intentionally make relationship-building the top priority. Let's face it, connecting with every student every day is not an easy task, however it is an essential that we all must strive to attain within our profession.

Hallway Heroes

Cook et al. (2018) showed the simple act of greeting students at the door produces a 20 percent increase in academic engagement and a nine percent decrease in disruptive behavior. But, why? Jumping back to our hallway heroes mentioned earlier and diagnosing their daily greetings with students is the perfect starting place for diving deeper into the importance of classroom connection. What is it about these personalized interactions that is so impactful?

When looking at the welcome routines more closely, we see they all have three common ingredients: eye contact, a smile, and personal recognition.

Eye Contact. Every handshake begins with eye-contact. This often-overlooked action is a necessity. The simple act communicates to the student, "I notice you." Feeling noticed is the first step to feeling important.

A Smile. Nothing fancy needed next, just a simple smile. Not only is smiling emotionally contagious, but the underlying meaning behind the upturn of the lips, has a powerful effect. This simple movement is an invitation to safety. It signals to the child that "you are safe here and I will protect you." Inside the child, knowing the most basic of all needs has been met, is released an immediate sense of relief. The student knows this is a positive place and one in which can be explored safely.

Personal Recognition. Sure, the fancy handshakes are cool, but it is the individualization of the morning greeting that is the icing on the connection cake. Acknowledging each child in a personalization manner screams loudly, "You are special and unique. You matter!" This is how each and every one of us, child or adult, wants, needs, and craves. To feel we matter and that we are cared for. Simply put, this trio of actions send students one incredibly powerful, yet clear message: "YOU MATTER!" And, whether adult or child, young or old, we all crave that feeling. We all have an internal need to feel important, loved, and connected.

Start Early

It is mid-August. Leslie had been up early that morning. Her nervous excitement left her sleepless. She had been waiting for this day for 2 months. Today was the day class lists would be posted at school. She couldn't wait to find out who her new teacher would be, and if any of her friends would be in her class. The thoughts raced through her head, "What would her teacher be like? Will the teacher like me? Will I like her? Will the teacher care about me as much as last year's teacher? What if none of my friends are in my class?"

Across town, Mrs. Epley, a third-grade teacher, was as eager about the start of the school year. Although the official start of the school year was still days away, she understood that a student's school year really begins the minute they find out who their teacher will be for the year. The time between learning who would lead them through the year and walking through the doors could seem like an eternity to some children. Not wanting the children in her class to waste a minute on negative thought or unnecessary worry, Mrs. Epley had a plan.

"Mrs. Epley, who is that?" Leslie wondered when she saw her new teacher's name. "I don't know anything about her." She headed home, walking, wondering, and worrying. The moment she got home, that all changed. Taped to the front door was a letter with her name on it. It was a personalized note from her new teacher. Leslie opened the letter and knew right away that it would be a great year.

Mrs. Epley used the letter to not only introduce herself, but to let Leslie and every other every child in her class know that she couldn't wait to get to know each one of them. She shared how she, too, was nervous about the start of the year, but would do everything she could to make it a great year. She let them know how excited she was to get to know each of them, including their likes, dislikes, and all the little things that made each one of them special. She went on to share that she had been preparing all summer for their arrival and how she would go out of her way to make learning relevant. She concluded by saying she couldn't wait to see them for the first time. In just a few short paragraphs, Leslie had learned a lot. But most importantly, she learned the one thing she really needed to know—that Mrs. Epley cared!

Friendly Confines

When students feel comfortable and relaxed in a particular teacher's classroom, they are more energized, engaged, and motivated to learn. The feelings of belonging and relatedness created, sparks student enthusiasm, interest, and willingness to participate in academic tasks. Furrer and Skinner (2003) stated, "It seems to be more fun for children to be involved in activities with people that they like and by whom they feel liked in return. Relatedness may also buffer against negative emotions, minimizing feelings of boredom, anxiety, pressure, or frustration" (p. 158).

In classrooms where relationships are strong, student success is evident at every turn. Caring teachers are approachable, empathetic, and generally interested in the well-being of their students.They listen attentively to students concerns, providing emotional support and, when appropriate, taking steps to alleviate challenges that students find stressful (Ferguson et al., 2015).

Energized by relationships, students are empowered. Knowing they have someone at their side promotes a sense of emotional security and confidence. This leads students to tackle challenging goals, reflect upon and use feedback, and maintain motivation when experiencing setbacks. Close and supportive teacher-student relationships greatly enhance student outcomes at all levels.

Unfortunately, poor relationships with teachers, as defined by a lack of closeness, leave students feeling like a visiting team member in front of a hostile crowd. Lack of rapport between the teacher and child greatly impacts student outcomes. In these situations, the failure to connect is highly correlated to decreases in critical thinking, social connection between students, grades, behavior in class, student alienation, affection from school, and increases in dropout rates (Cornelius-White, 2007).

The worst part is that it is not just that these bad experiences have more impact on student outcome than good ones do (Roorda et al., 2011), but these negative effects linger. The cascading effect of the negative relationships and children's externalizing behaviors become stronger over time (Roorda et al., 2011), whereas positive aspects of teacher-student relationships have short-term effects. Overcoming negative teacher-student interactions take time and repeated effort by the teacher to repair and rebuild. Children have a particularly hard time getting past such experiences. Based on these findings, teachers must focus daily on building and rebuilding connections with students in order to provide the student optimal learning conditions.

Together these results provide important insight into when and why a focus should be placed on developing stronger bonds between teachers and students. One would think connections would be easily fostered by educators; unfortunately, quality connections in the classroom are more the exception than the rule. So, where do we begin?

Connection Creators

Connection is about communicating safety and respect; it's as simple and as complex as that. There are certain actions in the classroom that teachers can take to not only increase the speed, but also the strength of their connections.

Know Each Child's Name. Teachers need to know each child's name and use it while speaking to them in the classroom. I know, this sounds simple, but my evidence reveals that it is not. While researching for this book, I interviewed dozens of students about their experiences in the classroom. I asked them what teachers did that they liked, what they didn't like, and what could be done differently. Shockingly, "Call me by my name" came up over and over again, especially from students in grades six through 12.

My own daughter shared with me how frustrated she felt when one of her junior high teachers said, "Hey, you in the blue shirt, you read next." Seriously, I was shocked. I don't care if a teacher has two, 20, or 200 students, they should make it a priority to know all their students' names. It may take a little more time and effort if you interact with hundreds of students a day, but it is possible. As part of an action research project, one graduate student of mine tried a variety of different memory aides to try and speed up this process. She found taking a picture of each child and writing down one fact about each, then reviewing the pictures for 30 minutes each night until all were memorized, worked extremely well. A physical education teacher who taught next to me for 4 years needed a financial incentive to sharpen his focus. He promised to give any student whose name he didn't know after the first week of school a nickel. Yes, it was only five cents, but as he told me, it adds up if not focused. These little tricks may take a little extra effort, but they are more than doable. Knowing a child's name matters. Our names make us unique. When we feel unique, we feel special. "Hey, you!" is never going to motivate a student.

Be Credible. Kids can tell a fake from a mile away. They know immediately whether a teacher is genuine or not. When teachers aren't credible, students won't give them the time of day. Why would any student waste time on someone who isn't as invested in them as they are invested in their curriculum. Credibility in the classroom is contingent upon four factors (McCroskey, Valencic, & Richmond, 2004):

1. Trust is the first of these, and the most important. Unfortunately, many teachers make the assumption, since they are adults, trust will be given to them automatically. Nothing can be further from the truth. Trust develops slowly and is earned daily. Brene Brown (2015) likened trust to a marble jar, explaining that each time we demonstrate vulnerability, we add a marble. Over time, the jar fills and students begin to believe that their teachers care about their success and have their best interests at heart. Teachers can take the fast track to a trusting relationship by admitting to not knowing everything, acknowledging when they make mistakes, not throwing around false praise, and showing individual interest in each child. By attending student activities outside the school day and asking students about their lives outside the classroom, teachers show they care. These little moves in the moment are marbles in the trust jar.

2. The second component of credibility is competence. While interviewing a 17-year-old high school student on this topic, he was pretty blunt, stating, "Teachers need to know their stuff. Plain and simple, I want to know if they got game." Students know if the teacher is prepared or not, organized or not. This goes beyond knowing the subject matter. Teachers need to be able to communicate both academic and behavioral expectations clearly, as well as know how to help students when struggling. This is of particular importance during the middle and high school years, when students begin to become more aware of things like this. As the interviewee above stated, "Kids can see right through a poser."

3. The third aspect of credibility is immediacy. Immediacy in the classroom refers to the sense of urgency one brings to teaching. When teachers make it clear to students that the subject matter and learning is important, students begin to internalize that belief. Personal stories about how they have used the subject matter knowledge in their own lives allows students to see the value in the learning. The key is to share quick quips that inspire and inform, not long-winded stories that bore and disengage the students.

4. The fourth feature of credibility is charisma. As a former superintendent I worked for was fond of saying, "Great teachers have a little Elvis in them." Credible teachers don't need to sing or dance, but they need to be able to hold the students' attention. They must be able to convey enthusiasm and passion for learning. When they do so, they are able to ignite a similar energy within students.

Self-Disclosure. Students love learning about their teachers and hearing about their lives outside of school. When teachers open up and share information such as personal anecdotes about themselves, who their spouse or significant other is, what they like to do, where they like to travel or how they spend their off hours, students feel special. Those momentary glimpses behind the curtain make students' feel they have a significant role to play in the teacher's world.

The most basic of all personal disclosures, and a potential "must" in every classroom, is the "Me" Board, or a simple bulletin board area filled with pictures of the teacher; this board may illustrate where she went to school, her pets, her friends, her spouse/significant other, or other loved ones. When students see these visuals, they begin to see the teacher in a new light. They begin to connect to the images and develop a sense of empathy.

Figure 2. Example of "Me" Board.

One of my favorite examples of personal disclosure is when teachers set aside a block of time each month for a "Passion Period." Dozens of schools around the country allow their teachers to spend one period each month teaching students about themselves. If a teacher loves cooking, she can teach about that. A teacher that loves to play the guitar may spend 20 minutes teaching the students how to play and sharing what was learned in the process. Sure, this is a period of "lost" curriculum content time, but administrators have cited that what they get back in teacher-student relationship development is well worth it. Additionally, many have said when teachers are in the midst of teaching their passion, they exhibit some of their best instruction—a double whammy.

"Mini-courses" are an offshoot of Passion Period and another great way of letting kids see what teachers are passionate about. On a half-day of school or a day before a holiday, high schools and middle schools often run abbreviated schedules. Rather than try and press through a normal day of instruction, these schools have staff volunteers teach a mini-course on a special topic of interest. After all teachers have determined a topic to teach, students from across grade levels throughout the building sign up to attend the new mini-courses. Staff love the change of pace and the opportunity to teach something different, while students love getting to meet new teachers and learn about things not taught in the typical school curriculum.

Whether it's Passion Period, mini-courses, or traditional "Me" Boards, students feel a huge sense of belonging when teachers reveal their human side.

Similarities. My son was 5 years old, and we were watching television together. An advertisement popped up on the screen for a new police drama that would start that fall. My son turned to me and said, "Dad, I bet you would like that show." I was curious as to why he would think I would be interested. I said, “What makes you think I would like that show?” He replied, “Because the main character is a cool, bald guy, and so are you.” After relishing in the fact my son thought I was cool, I thought more deeply about what he was saying. People connect when they realize they have things in common with others. I would later come to understand the magnitude of this when reading a Harvard research study by Dr. Hunter Gehlbach and colleagues (2015). These researchers found that when teachers and students perceive themselves as similar to one another, closer teacher-student relationships are developed, and academic achievement gains are shown (Gehlbach et al., 2015). The boosts in achievement were particularly noteworthy amongst black and Latino students, showing a 60 percent reduction in the achievement gap.

Figure 3. Twin Day: Similarities with the teacher.

The free 15-minute “Get to Know You” survey developed by Gehlbach et al. (2015) is available online from Panorama Education. The results inform students immediately on their similarities with their teacher and act as a great way to start conversations and begin building connections in the classroom.

Other teachers choose to use more traditional methods. When I taught, one-to-one technology and online surveys weren’t available options. For me it was brief one on one conversations with each child. Over the course of the first few days, I would sit down with pencil and clipboard in hand to fill out my “31 Chart.” This chart was nothing more than a three-column chart in which I had the students’ names listed, three new things I learned about each child from the conversation, and one commonality we shared. I would highlight what we had in common and use it over time as a lead to learn more.

Regardless of methodology, learning and reinforcing the things that we have in common with students speeds up the relationship-building process.

Power Leads. In Broadcasting Happiness, positive psychologist and former CBS news anchor Michelle Gielan (2015) discussed the impact of using power phrases to start conversation. Gielan recommended that teachers use power leads like, “I noticed…, “I was thinking about you…”, “I’m impressed with…” or “You’re making progress on…” to let students know they are cared about (2015). These messages, like greetings at the door, let students know how much we value them and how important they are in our lives.

Connection Killers

> *As there are distinct actions that create connections in the classroom, there are several that immediately kill connection. Relationships can erode in a heartbeat, and some of these behaviors empty the "marble jar" in a hurry.*

Sarcasm. Plain and simple there is no place in the classroom for sarcasm. Sarcasm, as defined by Webster, is "a sharp and often satirical or ironic utterance designed to cut or give pain." Yes, pain is the problem. Although teachers do not deliberately use sarcasm to cause pain, the reality is that it happens. It happens because the young developing mind is often not adept enough in the situation to discern whether the little truth hidden within the sarcasm is a veiled message. While the giver may view the sarcastic remark as just that, often times the recipient is unsure.

A perfect example of accidental sarcasm occurred with my daughter. As an introvert, she tends to sit back and let the relationships come to her. After several weeks of school, despite having a very gregarious and outgoing teacher, she didn't yet feel a connection. One day, during math class, the teacher came up to my daughter and asked her if she had finished her work. She replied that she was still working on it. In an attempt at sarcasm and humor, he said aloud, "Well, come on slacker. Let's get it done." OH NO! That was the wrong thing to say. That message tore her down. Again, not his intent, but he didn't know her well enough to understand that the term "slacker" struck a chord. She was the type of girl who works tirelessly to get stuff done a day before it is due, to always be prepared. To then be called a "slacker" was earth-shattering. She came home that night and cried for an hour—not only because her teacher had called her that, but thinking other kids had heard it and would label her in such a manner also. The frustration lasted for the remainder of the year, as the voice of her teacher calling her slacker played in her head over and over like a broken record. This comment caused Maddie, as well as several of her friends, to close up even tighter.

I obviously felt terrible for my daughter, but I also felt bad for the teacher. Again, he meant well, but he learned the hard way what happens when sarcasm backfires. Sadly, he is not alone, this happens hundreds, if not thousands, of times a day in classrooms throughout the country. Instead of increasing the levels of psychological safety in the classroom, the classroom can become a place where teasing and sarcasm are ongoing and students sit worrying all class period long whether they will be the next victim.

Lack of empathy. Empathy is an incredibly important characteristic in a teacher as it fosters a sense of care and support. Too often, teachers become consumed in the content they teach, feeling a rush to teach it all NOW! "True empathy begins with listening—taking the time not just to hear, but to understand what someone else is thinking and feeling" (Hoerr, 2017, p. 35). A lack of empathy signals a lack of care. Students in need depend on an empathetic ear to process their feelings and feel loved, understood, and safe.

Teacher's Pets. It is natural to just click with some students. We have all had those students where the connection was automatic. No effort was needed, it was just there. Researchers have concurred that teachers, like everyone else, have preferences for students who are like them in personality, background and experience (Morganett, 2001). As personally rewarding as these relationships are, we need to be careful that students don't know who the favorites are. Once students see who the teacher's pet is, the jockeying begins. Many students will try and complete for that top honor or slink to the back of the pack, writing the teacher off for not caring about them. In the words of Todd Whitaker (2013), "In the great teacher's classroom, every student thinks they are the favorite!"

Public Shaming. On the flip side of the automatic connections, there are automatic disconnections. There are certain students that we are going to really have to work hard to get to know. As Manny Scott (2018) said during a conference keynote, "It's easy to build relationships with people who are just like you, but how do you build relationships with people who are different than you?". These kids are going to take time and ongoing efforts to develop a bond. Additionally, when faced with students who are more demanding, teachers need to draw heavily upon their self-regulatory skills in order to not "flip their lids." Avoiding singling students out in front of peers is a must. This is not easy. I would love some mulligans in order to go back and do things different when I was in the classroom. But because I can't, I will try and explain as clearly as I can: children only feel as safe in a classroom as the worst behaved child is treated. Let me repeat that. Children only feel as safe in a classroom as the worst behaved child is treated.

I once thought students in my class would see what I saw: a misbehaving student who needed to get his act together. Unfortunately, even if they agreed that the rule breaker was out of line, inside they were thinking, "If it can happen to him, it can happen to me." All this did was damage the feelings of safety and cause distrust.

The impact of a teacher yelling or scolding a student in front of peers has a continued negative ripple effect. At the elementary age, children make judgments about their classmates based on perceptions of how the target child interacts with and is perceived by the teacher. Acceptance and rejection by peers is based upon acceptance and rejection of the teacher (Fredricksen & Rhodes, 2004). If the teacher likes you, chances are your peers will too. This changes as students age. For older students, although they pay close attention to teacher child interactions, they have a tendency to side with the student rather than the teacher. The impacts of such negative individual relationships affect the dynamics of the entire class.

Hierarchy. Following on the heels of favorites and shaming, a pattern begins to emerge. When there are winners and losers in the classroom, no one really wins. Hierarchical structures in the classroom can have catastrophic effects. Examples of such things include classroom behavior charts, posted classroom grades, reading incentives gone wrong, or other frameworks that label students into categories. In these classrooms, competition to be king of the mountain and stay there becomes the goal rather than an increased love of learning. Wang and Holcombe (2010) found that competitive classroom environments decrease student participation and undermine a sense of belonging. Why? The constant state of comparing oneself to another and becoming self-judging as to whether one is good, bad or great, hampers the development of self-esteem. The key then is to flatten class systems. Designing a classroom environment based on fairness and providing equal access for all students to opportunity closes achievement gaps and leads to decreases in bullying.

Connection Mindset

Connection is not a single act; it is a mindset. It is the daily execution of ensuring students feel safe, secure and loved within the classroom. Without explicitly setting aside time for relationship development, great things will not be possible in the classroom. It has been said, the deeper the foundation, the higher the building. In this situation, the deeper the connections, the higher the possibilities of student success.

Reflect/Rethink/Refine

- *What is your daily welcome ritual and what message do you feel it sends to your students?*
- *What is your primary method of teaching students about you, as a person?*
- *Think of an example of when you were a victim of sarcasm. How did it make you feel?*
- *What are three specific actions you can take to create greater connections with your students?*
- *How might you explain the impact of hierarchy in the classroom to your peers?*

3 CHAPTER

OBSESS OVER THE PRESS

Maddie's Message:
I know I matter when my teacher pushes me to do things I didn't think I could do.

It was 11:00 AM on the first day of summer track camp. It was my opportunity to teach this group of fourth through eighth graders how to run hurdles. I had a half-dozen collapsible hurdles set up at various heights, and I couldn't wait to show them how much fun this event could be.

The first boy was up, the 24-inch hurdle ahead in the lane. He jumped it with little effort. I urged him to try a higher height, raised the hurdle to 27 inches, and off he went. Again, no problem, but he was getting nervous. Once more I challenged him to go higher, now at 30 inches, my standard for the end of the week. No problem at that height either. Finally, at 33 inches, well outside of his comfort zone, I urged him on. Although his form started to break down, his adrenaline carried him over the obstacle. Each time, his pride grew as he came back to the starting line. There we stopped, and it was the next child's turn.

Hayley, although short in stature, was anxious for her turn. She took off toward the 24-inch height, barely clearing the bar. I was impressed, as was she. Afraid I might kill her enthusiasm and possibly scare the others if Hayley was unsuccessful on her next attempt, I moved to the next girl. This continued until each child had a turn.

At the next water break, I looked over and saw Hayley sitting by herself on the bleachers. Tears were welling up in her eyes. I sat down beside her to see what was wrong. After some prodding, she said, "You don't like me, do you?" I was shocked; I barely knew her. I quickly said, "Of course I like you. What would give you the idea I don't?"

In a moment that is still etched in my memory, she looked at me and said, "If you liked me, you would have challenged me like you did the first boy. You would have pushed me and encouraged me to jump higher." Wow! I didn't know what to say.

Looking back, I now see in that moment, I wasn't being a Significant Sally. I was being a Chris the Camp Counselor. I had lowered my expectations for Hayley based upon a fear of her failure. I so badly wanted her to feel good about the event, I didn't want to take the chance that she might experience struggle and suffer physical or emotional pain.

This fear of mine was one generated by unconscious stereotyping. I inferred, due to her height, and possibly her gender, that she may not experience success at the next level. Rather than allowing her the opportunity and realizing it could become a motivating factor, like it did for the first child, I held her back, which sent her the message that I did not have confidence in her abilities. Additionally, she took from what I had done an even worse message—that the reason I didn't push her to meet a higher challenge was because I didn't care. These two thoughts are terrible for relationships and have potentially devastating effects on student growth and accomplishment.

That event changed my teaching and coaching forever. From that day forward, I would be intentional about ensuring all students understood that I believed they were capable of great things and because I cared so much about them, I would push them out of their comfort zone in order for then to experience success.

Stereotyping in the Classroom

The human brain has developed over thousands of years to keep us alive. In order to ensure our safety, it quickly sifts through the vast amount of information that we take in and sorts it based on our prior knowledge and experiences. This is of huge advantage in helping us more quickly respond to threat. While this is very beneficial in times of crisis, it can negatively impact our interactions with others. Responding in this manner often causes us to ignore differences in people, consciously or unconsciously generalizing based upon things that may or not be true, resulting in hard-to-let-go-of stereotypes.

Once a generalization occurs, our brain again goes into default mode trying to determine if our initial assessment of the situation is accurate. Searching all additional incoming information, we inherently hold onto information that confirms what we believe to be true. This reinforces our initial beliefs and dismisses other data that we take in.

This process, known as confirmation bias, makes us highly susceptible to biases and stereotypes developed over time. The thoughts we have about others leads us to treat them accordingly. Our actions then cause them to develop certain beliefs about us. In Hayley's situation, this was evidenced by her thinking I didn't want to challenge her. Which, then resulted in her inferring I didn't like her—a reverse confirmation bias or stereotype based on her reality.

Luckily, I was able to intervene in time and change that narrative. Had I not, the cycle would have continued. She would have begun to act as if I didn't care about her or have confidence in her and would spend time searching for evidence to prove that point. The resulting beliefs would have impacted not only how she viewed me, but herself as well; potentially leading her to questioning her own abilities and whether there was something wrong with her. Self-fulfilling prophecies like this can have devastating effects on student social, emotional, and academic success.

Self-Fulfilling Prophecies and Expectations

Whether it be race, gender, income level, social class, language proficiency, or learning difference, all educators hold internal biases and beliefs that impact how children in their classrooms are treated. These beliefs are confirmed or enhanced based upon student action during the first weeks of school, initial assessment data, anecdotal comments, and insight from previous teachers. Students are then ranked, sorted, classified and categorized. Be it on paper or just in teacher's minds, it is important to remember that anytime there is a level or label placed on a student, we face the chance of limiting learning. To be blunt, once a label is affixed to the forehead of a child, it is almost impossible to remove.

Further, teachers, consciously or unconsciously, begin to use this initial leveling to make growth judgments about particular students and groups of students, projecting growth for the year. Statements such as, "Wow, this is a low group, gonna be a long year" or "Man, I have some high kids… I will have to step up my game" are often heard in teacher's lounges in mid-September each year. Although it is human nature to have these thoughts, these class-wide statements are the start of the vicious cycle known as "self-fulfilling prophecy".

Although "damaging" for some students, the self-fulfilling prophecy can be positive for students seen as "talented." Jennifer Lee, author of *The Asian American Achievement Paradox*, tells the story of a young Vietnamese girl. Self-described as "not very smart," she earned C grades throughout junior high. But, for some reason the child was placed in AP courses when she entered high school. Teachers thinking, based upon her last name, she was placed in the wrong class, advanced her to the more challenging course level. She was provided high expectations and challenge by her teachers, as well as modeling from more determined classmates. She thrived, earning a 4.3 grade point average and admittance into a prominent university. Lee went on to say this situation was not unique. She found thousands of cases where students, when pressed academically at very high levels, met or exceeded expectations.

Henry Ford once said, "Whether you think you can or you think you can't, you're right." We need to ensure students think they can learn at high levels. When students believe they can achieve, they will find a way. Further, we need to believe every student can, and will learn. When we do, we are more likely to design learning experiences and instructional practices that ensure success as the natural end result.

Challenge Mindset

Ghandi once said, "*Your beliefs become your thoughts, your thoughts become your words, your words become your actions, and your actions become your habits.*"

Teachers' beliefs about their students and how they might perform in a classroom have tremendous effect on subsequent student attitudes, performance and achievement. Courageous teachers know that it isn't student ability that determines success, but teacher challenge and the accompanying mindsets. They know all children can, and will be successful, and they put specific actions and habits in place to ensure success occurs.

Dweck et al. (2014) suggested, "Effective teachers and schools understand that it is through challenge that students learn and achieve over time," and "whereas effective teachers and schools challenge their students with high performance standards, less effective ones cater to the presumed limitations of their students by setting low standards" (p. 22).

Courageous teachers uphold the challenge throughout the lesson, never giving into the pull of their heartstrings when seeing students struggle. They understand that struggle is needed to grow. They understand that academic press is the key to student success.

Press: High and Low

Many schools and educators talk about high expectations and their ability to challenge students, but few actually are able to walk the talk. It's not because of a lack of know-how, but a lack of know-better.

Christine Rubie-Davies and her colleagues at the University of Auckland in New Zealand, arguably the world's leading authorities in the area of high expectations, have taken a close look at the habits of teachers. Based on her findings and my experiences, it is possible to develop a profile of two contrasting teachers: the low-press teacher and the high-press teacher.

Low-Press Teachers	High-Press Teachers
Extrinsic motivation	Internal motivation
Ability groups	Flexible groups
Little interaction with mixed ability peers	Work in variety of pairings
Student responsibility for learning	Shared responsibility for learning
Low level tasks	Challenging tasks
Closed questioning	Open-ended questioning
Directive	Facilitative
More teacher talk	More student talk
Assess for level	Assess for needs
Limited feedback	Frequent feedback
Abundance of procedural directions	Clearly established routines
Punitive behavior management	Positive behavior management

Figure 4. Adapted from Rubie-Davies and Peterson (2011).

Different views of student abilities lead to different levels of curricular intensity. Teachers with lower expectations design less cognitively-demanding lessons. They do not hold students accountable for learning throughout lessons, and monitor students' progress less frequently. This often results in teachers spending more time than necessary reinforcing and repeating concepts, even when students may already have learned the material.

The high-press classroom is quite different. High-press teachers recognize that every child is unique and value all abilities. They realize the common denominator of success is the high level of academic press they provide to students, and monitor student progress closely, providing tailored support to each learner as needed. Further, they understand their expectations directly impact students' motivation, self-esteem, and performance.

When teachers create a psychosocial climate that provides challenging learning experiences and clear learning goals, students are more likely to respond with high intrinsic motivation and a determination to be successful in their learning (Weinstein & McKown, 1998).

When our feelings about student abilities change, so does how we teach. If we believe they are low, we teach them low. It is as simple as that.

The Seven Ps of Press

Teachers who genuinely care about their students care about pushing them to exceed in all aspects of learning. Upholding the challenge means pressing students gently and consistently throughout their learning journey. It means standing side-by-side with students when they are intellectually intimidated, and not letting them off the hook just so they feel more comfortable. Sympathy syndrome deprives students of the cognitive conflict needed for them to grow. The social, emotional, and academic skills developed during those times of struggle, are the skills students will rely on during college and career. These, therefore, are opportunities that teachers must not deprive their students from having.

For students to optimally learn, they must be pressed in seven areas: preparedness, participation, ponder, proficiency, perseverance, progress, and positivity.

Preparedness. In order to be cognitively challenged, students must first be in attendance and prepared. Poor attendance negatively impacts student results at all ages. When students are chronically absent, the courageous teacher doesn't blame the child or parent; instead the teacher reinforces the importance of being in attendance and reaches out to let the child know they were missed. Simply saying, "We missed you while you were gone" or "We were thinking of you while you were sick" conveys how much you care that the child is there. I have been amazed at the impact that this one-sentence intervention has on reducing chronic absenteeism.

Students should also be required to bring all necessary materials to class. Although seemingly obvious, the difference here is how the courageous teacher handles missing work. For example, the penalty for not doing their homework, is doing the homework. A zero in the gradebook or a lecture might make the teacher feel good, but it doesn't teach the child the importance of follow-through. Educators, therefore, must hold students responsible, as it is the responsibility that more closely ensures learning occurs.

Part of being ready to learn requires students to know how to act in the classroom. Much learning time in classrooms is lost because students are not consistently held accountable for classroom expectations. Teachers must teach, reteach and remind all students of classroom expectations and routines and insist all students follow those guidelines. Too often, bias shows in this area as students with infrequent infractions are let off the hook and rarely reprimanded while the same behaviors displayed result in a reprimand for the "frequent flier". Remember, the high challenge teacher shares responsibility for a child's success at all times.

Participation. The hours that teachers spend crafting and engineering the most rigorous curriculum and instructional plans are rendered useless if only half the students get the opportunity to take part in the lesson. Allensworth et al. (2018) wrote, "Teachers are more often encouraged to focus on 'what' is being learned rather than grapple with why students are not fully participating in the process of learning" (p. 4).

Teachers must design ways for all students to participate in each lesson. Participation is the only way students can demonstrate what they know and are able to do. If the lesson is worth learning, it is worth educators spending the time to determine how child can be involved. One way to ensure students have a chance to interact with content is utilizing Kagan Cooperative Learning structures. Teachers use these structures to increase student engagement by grouping students in heterogeneous groups of four. Each group has equal representation from each learning level. Students are intentionally paired with peer models that help take their learning to the next level. Engagement is a given when students take part in this manner. Further, participation isn't determined on the basis of being an introvert or an extrovert; there are no "hogs and logs" when all are pressed to participate.

Another way to increase participation is to implement a no hand-raising policy. If a question is worth asking, it is worth every child answering. Teachers provide students processing time to answer the question privately (in their head), on paper, with a partner, or with the pack (table group), then have them report out. Once all students have answered the question in one of those four ways, the teacher can call on someone to answer. This process draws out student curiosity, as they want to hear how their answer compares to the other child's. In turn, this forces them to do higher-level thinking. We have a responsibility to get students in the game and then urge them onward.

Ponder. Now that we have all students involved in the process of learning, we must increase the level of questioning asked within the classroom. The low challenge classroom is full or simple yes/no, recall and regurgitated lower level, closed-ended questions. BORING!

Courageous teachers require rigorous thought. They expect students to think deeply and explain their reasoning behind every answer. They take time to develop the metacognitive skills students need as they tackle college or career. They push students to prove their thinking, rather than just to provide a response.

Socratic seminar activities are one tool that teachers can use to enhance student opportunities to think critically. A form of debate, this method forces participants to research, evaluate, connect, and integrate ideas. I have seen students who are at times not particularly engaged in learning shine when drawn into this type of discussion.

Every child deserves to be intellectually challenged, not just the "low" kids. Too often our most talented students are never challenged until they get to college and then once faced with the challenge, don't know how to respond. We owe it to them to interact with the material and stretch their thinking as much as we do their peers.

Proficiency. While ponder is about the process of thinking deeply, proficiency is about the level of student's success on grade level curriculum. All students should be exposed to rigorous content and be provided the scaffolds needed to reach success. In the courageous teacher's classroom, there is a floor, but no ceiling. The floor in this classroom is grade level content. Courageous teachers are always pressing students to increase proficiency beyond their current level.

Too many students graduate from high school without the knowledge and skills necessary to succeed in college or career. According to the *Opportunity Myth Report* (2018), research conducted by The New Teacher Project (2018) on over 4,000 children in five diverse school systems found that students spend the majority of their day without access to four key resources: grade-appropriate assignments, strong instruction, deep engagement, and teachers who hold high expectations. Their findings revealed that students of color, those from low-income families, English language learners, and students with mild to moderate disabilities have even less access. The good news was that given the supports, students who started the year below grade level, were able to close achievement gaps with peers by 6 months.

Grade-appropriate content is crucial for student success. Students must be provided access to the critical concepts and essential understandings required for their age. Clear goals should be outlined via learning intentions and success criteria. High-press teachers then present students with tasks that require them to apply those concepts in real-world contexts and press them to become proficient.

Once instruction is complete, standards-based assessments are utilized to provide information to the teacher on student understanding. Aligning the rigor of the assessment to the rigor of the standards can be a daunting task but is necessary to ensure students meet expectations.

Although utilizing academically challenging content is essential for learning, raising the level of challenge in a class without changing the amount of support students receive is more likely to cause students to fail and receive lower grades (Allensworth et al., 2018). Teachers must provide appropriate scaffolds and supports for each student. Knowing each student well, and what each needs to learn, is a hallmark of the high-care, high-press teacher.

Perseverance. Watch students outside of the classroom. Whether on the couch playing video games with friends or on an athletic field, you will see children experiencing struggle and overcoming obstacles all the time. Why then, don't we see these similar efforts placed in the classroom? The answer is simple: perseverance is task-specific and situation-dependent.

The University of Chicago's Camille Farrington (2013) argued that academic perseverance is a learnable skill because it applies to the specific context of persevering at academic tasks. Farrington et al. (2012) stated, "Students can be influenced to demonstrate perseverant behaviors- such as persisting at academic tasks, seeing big projects through to completion, and buckling down when schoolwork gets hard, in response to certain classroom contexts and under particular psychological conditions" (p. 24).

As educators, we need to provide students with the opportunity to struggle and then teach them how to remain engaged in learning despite obstacles, setbacks and distractions that get in the way. The ability to persist through the trials and tribulations and remain focused on the goal is key to both short-term and long-term success.

The high-press, high-caring teacher utilizes grade-level plus content to push students out of their comfort zone, yet remains there at their side, supporting them and not allowing them to give up. This is the crucial moment in education, the moment that separates the best from the rest. This is the moment of truth for educators: do we stand alongside them gently pushing them through that period of productive struggle knowing when they come out the other side, they will feel the confidence and motivation, take on more challenging adventures, or do we make things easier for them by lessening their load and rescuing them from experience? This is where I failed Hayley, but will never fail another.

Progress. The development of self-regulatory skills such as self-assessing, self-monitoring, and goal-setting is one of an educator's most important goals. The key behind these processes is one's ability to determine where they are at in their learning journey.

Too often, today's classrooms do not provide students opportunities to monitor their own progress. Instead, students just sit and wait for their teachers to let them know how they have done. This can be defeating.

Students, like all people, thrive on seeing their progress. One only needs to watch a child spend a few minutes playing Fortnite to see this firsthand. Amabile and Kramer, authors of *The Progress Principle* (2011), cited that "real progress triggers positive emotions like satisfaction, gladness, even joy. It leads to a sense of accomplishment and self-worth as well as positive views of the work" (p. 68). Further, knowing what they have already accomplished motivates learners to go further.

Personalized goal setting can be used to motivate students. The WOOP Goal Process, developed by Gabriele Oettingen and defined later in this book, is an excellent tool for the classroom. This step-by-step strategy calls upon students to set a goal, think about a positive outcome related to the goal, identify obstacles that may get in their way of accomplishing it, and develop a plan for overcoming those obstacles. The frequent use of this method helps instill in students the knowledge that they have the ability to make progress when they challenge themselves.

Positivity. It is natural for students to get frustrated and want to give up. It is important that teachers push students to stay mentally positive throughout their learning. Viewing one's self as positive and having an optimistic outlook on learning helps students succeed. Too many students view situations as win or loss. Motivational expert John C. Maxwell is famous for saying, "sometimes you win and sometimes you learn." This is the motto of the high-press classroom.

Teachers are responsible for cultivating a growth mindset amongst their students. Throwing the word "yet" on the end of a statement, however, doesn't make for a growth mindset. Working diligently with students to realize the goal of learning isn't "to prove" but "to improve." This is what courageous teachers do.

Overarching Message

The greater the challenge a teacher places on a student, the greater the importance of the relationships between the two. When teachers consistently communicate the academic press for understanding they are placing on students, it is done because they care for and believe in the child, student motivation will never lack.

> ***"Every child deserves a champion: an adult who will never give up on them, who understands the power of connection and insists they become the best they can possibly be."***
>
> ------------------------------
>
> **Rita Pierson, Educator**

Reflect/Rethink/Refine

- *How do you currently press students to excel in each of the 7 Ps?*
- *How might you address habits you have that fall under those of a low press teacher?*
- *What can you do to press all students to participate in lessons?*
- *How do you respond when students give less than their best effort?*
- *How can you and your colleagues work to avoid common stereotypes and biases in the classroom?*

UNLEASH CLARITY

CHAPTER 4

Maddie's Message:
I know I matter when my teacher makes sure I understand what I need to learn.

Alissa was in her fourth year as a high school biology teacher. Having been a straight-A student throughout high school and college, she had never experienced struggle before in a classroom. She didn't think teaching would be easy, but she never imagined it would be this challenging. She thought her enthusiasm and passion for the subject would lead to her success, but this wasn't the case. She could sense by the look in her students' eyes and the feeling in her gut that something was missing.

Not sure what to do, she turned to her school's instructional coach for guidance. Her coach suggested that Alissa videotape a few of her lessons to get a better idea of what was happening in the classroom. Reluctantly, she agreed to the videotaping, recording over a dozen different lessons that week. She then spent time watching each lesson closely, taking notes and reflecting.

Monday morning arrived, and she sat down with her coach to debrief. She described how eye-opening the experience had been as she walked her coach through a typical lesson. She discussed how she started each lesson by reviewing the learning targets on the board, touched upon success criteria, and began teaching, providing details throughout. She noted that on most occasions, the students seemed confused as to what they were learning and what she was teaching. She felt she had so much to cover, she didn't have time to slow down and wait for them. "Besides," she said, "It's their responsibility to be good learners."

The instructional coach paused Alissa, and said, "Alissa, how do your students learn best? What do they need to be successful?"

Alissa stopped dead in her tracks. She realized in that moment that she had become so focused on what she needed to teach, that she had not slowed down long enough to get to know those she was teaching.

Not What, but Who First

In today's educational landscape, the scenario above is all too common. With all the curricular changes that come and go, many educators have become so fixated on the *"what"* of teaching, the *"how"* and most importantly the *"who"* are often placed on the back burner. *What* curriculum needs to be taught and *what* ways we use to ensure students know *what* is being assessed is important, yet failing to focus on the who will not produce the outcomes educators strive for. It is only when we know the *who* that we can determine *how* students will learn the *what* best.

Without knowing their students well and knowing themselves well, educators around the globe are lost and confused as to why success is not occurring at a greater pace. The resulting confusion not only impacts current learning and motivation, but also relationships within the room.

In this chapter, we will examine ways in which teachers can oust not only their own confusion, but that of their students in order to produce greater success in today's classrooms. We will discuss the steps that educators can take to increase classroom clarity and provide several proven methods to enhance student achievement.

Who? Your Students

In order to teach effectively, teachers must have taken into consideration the unique attributes and needs of the children that appear in front of them each day. Without an in-depth understanding of each child, teachers develop instructional plans based upon their own needs rather than those of the children, or generalize instruction based upon the "typical" child of the age they teach. If 25 years in education has taught me anything, it is that there is no such thing as "typical." Every child is different, every child is special, and every child comes to us with his or her own unique STORY *(Strengths, Tendencies, Opportunities, Resources, and Yearnings).*

Strengths. Karen Pittman, President and CEO of the Forum for Youth Investment, stated that "building on students' strengths is what great teachers, great parents, great youth workers, and great mentors do. They create environments in which young people feel comfortable owning and bringing in the skills and values they have and working on the skills they still need." Capitalizing on students' strengths within the classroom, then, is about taking the focus off what students cannot do, and instead placing the focus on what they can do. It is about teachers recognizing and utilizing the things students do well as springboards toward accomplishing items where more persistence is required.

Strengths-based education has proven to greatly increase student engagement and motivation in the classroom. A 2013 Gallup Student Poll surveyed over 100,000 students, finding that students who strongly agreed to the statement "My school is committed to building the strengths of each student" were 30 times more likely to be engaged at school than students who strongly disagreed with that statement. Knowing students' strengths matters.

How do we define student strengths? Dr. Lea Waters, author of The *Strength Switch* (2017), stated strengths must meet three criteria:

1. Strengths are positive qualities that energize us; that we perform well and choose often.
2. Strengths are built over time through our innate ability and dedicated effort.
3. Strengths are qualities recognized by others as praiseworthy.

Using strengths in students is not about developing, but unleashing. They are there; we just need to find ways to tap into them, and help students tap into them to create the fast pass to success.

There are multiple ways in which educators can assist students in identifying strengths. Online surveys like the free VIA Survey of Character Strengths, The Gallup Strength Finder, or those available at Thrively.com provide in-depth profiles on each student. This information can be utilized in numerous ways inside and outside the classroom. Teachers may also choose to ask their students simple questions such as those on the "MY STORY" worksheet to learn more about each child. Most importantly, however, is ensuring that each child, when asked, can identify his or her specific strengths. Our strengths become our identities. Students who begin seeing themselves through a strength lens feel empowered and emboldened. Conversely, students who never have the opportunity to recognize areas of strength, and have them celebrated by an adult, begin viewing themselves as lacking skills and never being good enough.

Tendencies. All people have certain ways in which they respond to learning and working in the classroom. Some students thrive on challenges set by others, while others withdraw when faced with external pressure. Some sit back quietly and do not speak until spoken to, while others are boisterous, outgoing, and extroverted in their interactions. Some children take copious notes while a teacher is talking, whereas others are able to recall the information delivered.

Whether it be a student's propensity toward always wearing certain types of clothing or making the same type of mistake over and over in math class, teachers can learn a lot from noticing patterns and trends displayed by their students. Each of these tendencies has been developed over time. Each is formed based upon the child's emotional state, confidence level, peer network, and past experiences, both inside and outside of the classroom. Each learner is different, but it is important that educators begin to recognize the patterns made visually in the classroom by their students.

Once discovered, teachers who have this valuable information about each child cannot help but act in ways that positively impact student learning.

Opportunities. Teachers are committed to helping students grow. We are good at identifying things that are wrong, and many have a box of red pens ready for just such occasions. The opposite of wrong is right. The opposite of a problem is a solution. We want to solve the problem and move onto solving the next. This mindset, however, creates a view of improvement which leads educators toward quick fixes. There is something the students can't do or that they are doing wrong, which needs to be fixed—problem solved. Unfortunately, the quick fix mentality is great for answering right and wrong questions, but ineffective for solving the more complex learning issues of students in need.

By reframing our perspective and beginning to view student need as opportunity, educators slow down their brains and begin to develop a mental model better able to process and solve complex challenges.

Too often, for example, we find a student who is struggling to multiply fractions. The teacher may think automatically that he doesn't have the skill or the will, and decide that he either needs to try harder or practice more. But we all know that it isn't that simple. A strong message from the findings of John Hattie's (2009) Visible Learning research is that when students do not learn, they do not need "more;" rather, they need different (p. 83).

When viewed with an opportunity and problem-solving lens, we begin to look at a larger variety of alternatives. Does the student need more time? Would alternate instructional techniques better meet the needs? Do they have the prerequisite knowledge to tackle problems such as these? What stage of learning is the student at?

Let's identify opportunities for students to grow and develop the best pathway forward and not the easiest for us.

Resources. Dictionary.com defines a resource as "a source of supply, support, or aid, especially one that can be readily drawn upon when needed." Knowing what resources each of our students can draw upon as they journey through our curriculum is vitally important.

Often overlooked, teachers can better assist students when they know what resources each child has in their imaginary backpack. This may be achieved by asking and answering the following questions:

- ❓ *Is there adequate food in the home?*
- ❓ *Is there someone at home to support them emotionally as well as academically?*
- ❓ *Does the student have quality friendships? A best friend? Role Models?*
- ❓ *Does the child have prior experiences or knowledge in the topic of study?*

- ❓ *Is the student new to the school or have they not gone to school for a while?*
- ❓ *Is the child able to study at home? Is Internet access available?*

Teachers should pay special attention to the first couple of bullet points listed above. In her book, Broadcasting Happiness, author Michelle Gielan (2015) utilized a very powerful acronym of her own: HALT. She discusses how all people, adult or child who are hungry, angry, lonely, or tired must have their basic needs met prior to learning or achieving at top levels. Put another way, as my colleague Tom Hierck stated, "If we don't take care of the Maslow stuff, we will never be able to do the Bloom stuff."

Yearnings. Keyontae was a fifth grade student of mine. He absolutely loved cars. He could look at a car and tell me the make, model, and year, as well as the type of engine inside. He spent every spare minute in the classroom either drawing cars, talking about cars, or reading a hot rod magazine. Knowing that this topic was so important to him, I not only had a quick way to talk to him and get to know him, but a motivational lever I could pull to more deeply engage him in learning.

Like Keyontae, when students are provided an opportunity to work on a topic they enjoy, they are more motivated, attentive, and willing to persevere when struggling. Why? Because they won't let struggle stand in the way of their curiosity. And when teachers like me know what students like Keyontae like and are passionate about, we can start making magic happen in the classroom.

While learning student interests and passions is important, teachers must go further. Students can't just work on passion projects all day long. There are times students will face instruction on topics they are not as fond of learning. With that in mind, teachers should begin to ascertain information regarding student learning preferences. Even acquiring information as to whether students prefer to work independently or in groups, assists teachers in creating a more optimal learning environment for each child.

The greatest mistake a teacher can make in the classroom is teaching as if everyone learns the same way. Recognizing and acknowledging every student has unique needs which require a unique learning path, is the first step to a teacher's success. Utilizing this information to make better instructional decisions enables a teacher to design and deliver the effective instruction needed so that each child can flourish.

Who? You

As Parker Palmer, author of *Courage to Teach* (1998), wrote, "Whoever our students may be, whatever the subject we teach, ultimately we teach who we are" (p.104). When I first read this quote during my first year of graduate school, I failed to recognize its importance. Now, over a dozen years later and after having seen hundreds of teachers in action, I realize the true power behind these words.

As much as every student has a story, so does every teacher. To illustrate this point, I often ask graduate students and workshop attendees to complete the Compass Points activity. This easy exercise gives teachers a quick, yet surprisingly accurate glimpse of themselves. Participants look at the four cardinal directions below and are asked to decide which best describes them as a teacher.

North: Northerners are all about action. They plunge right in and forge ahead. They hate waiting and want to get right after it. They like the big ideas, and if they agree with them, they jump on the bandwagon, often leading the way. They have a tendency, however, to move forward so quickly that they don't think things through. In the classroom, they see things so clearly, they often don't take the time to explain them fully to others.

South: Southerners are all about the love. They like to know everyone's feelings have been taken into account before moving forward. In the classroom, they want to make sure all voices have been heard before moving forward. They have a tendency to spend so much time coming to consensus on things, they never get started, or they are always running late.

East: Easterners want to see the big picture. They are highly speculative and love "what if?" questions. They must know their options before making a decision. In the classroom, they can present too many examples or too many viewpoints that some students become overwhelmed, leading to confusion.

West: The Westerners love their details. They want to know the who, what, when, where, and why before acting. If they are told to do an assignment, they want to know what font, which size, how many paragraphs, and so forth. This leads to an obsession that can halt their own movement and leave those around them worried that they have forgotten something.

Once participants have determined a style, they are asked to begin thinking of which group they find easiest to work with and which group they find most challenging to work with.

What I have found incredibly interesting over the years is how the vast majority of teachers, including myself, teach to their own direction. In other words, we have a tendency to teach in the way we learn best and teach in the subjects we are most passionate about learning. If we love details, we give students lots of details. If we feel that it is important to slow down to get everyone's perspective before moving forward, we do the same with our students. If we love science, we expect our students to love science. This is valuable insight, as we are almost all blind to this phenomenon. In many situations, what is causing a teacher's frustration and students' confusion is often a matter of perspective; we are viewing the world from one direction, instead of realizing that people are coming at the learning from many different ones.

We can build off of this exercise by quickly looking at Alissa's STORY.

Strengths. She loves science. She is hard-working, dedicated, and loves kids. She is a strong student and will work hard to excel.

Tendencies. She teaches like she learns. She is very verbal and detail-oriented. She talks too much.

Opportunities. She can incorporate more peer processing opportunities, rather than filling them with facts and details. Further, she can slow down instruction so that students can have a chance to ask questions.

Resources. She has many years of experience in science. She has an incredible instructional coach to support her.

Yearnings. She wants every student to love science as much as she does. She wants students to be successful.

Taking a deeper dive into Alissa's STORY provides some initial ideas as to why she may be feeling as frustrated as she has been in the classroom. In other words, having more clarity as to who we are as teachers, opens up opportunities to increase student understanding.

What?

Once teachers have a solid understanding of student needs and have self-reflected upon their own abilities as a teacher, they can turn their attention back to their curriculum. Having a deep understanding of the content one teaches, is imperative to not only student clarity, but one's own clarity.

Too often, with the demands of the profession today, teachers do not take the time to really understand what they are teaching. Too many teachers result in flipping to the next page in the teacher resource, proceeding to the next day's lesson without thought or buying a quick and easy lesson on Teachers Pay Teachers rather than taking the time to fully understand their subject well. This may get the teacher through the week, but it doesn't produce lasting achievement. Great learning opportunities for students must be planned out and build upon one another in a progression, getting more challenging as the days go on.

Herein lies the value of professional learning communities, instructional coaches, and great colleagues. These support systems are more critical to classroom success than ever before. Teaching is a team sport; no one can do it alone. By sitting down with their colleagues, teachers can begin laying out a clear progression of their content. What needs to be taught and the sequence of instruction is critical. At the same time, teams can discuss common student misconceptions while learning the materials.

What will instruction need to look like to create productive struggle and at what point might unproductive struggle set in? What background experiences do students have in this area? Are there vocabulary terms that need to be taught? Where are errors likely? Allocating more days of instruction or less based upon this information provides teachers a clearer picture of where they are going, which in turn speeds learning for their students. Setting aside the right amount of time for each lesson, rather than an equal amount of time per lesson, is crucial.

Teachers should keep their students at the forefront of their work during this planning phase. Taking notes on who may need more visual examples during a particular stage or who may need more guided practice is helpful in preparing for the journey ahead. Being cognizant of what it will take for each student to learn what is being taught increases our clarity on how to structure each day's activities.

How?

Drawing upon everything discussed in the chapter up to this point; knowing who our students are as learners, who we are as educators, and what content is to be taught, we are now able to begin designing effective daily lessons. This is where the rubber meets the road. We can do everything well up to this point, but if we are unable to pull it all together, uncertainty will creep into the minds of our students.

To enhance clarity in the classrooms, teachers must focus on each of the basic learning requirements. In order to learn anything, students need four things:

(a) Motivation, (b) Illustration, (c) Experimentation, and (d) Verification.

Motivation. All learning begins with motivation. Students don't act unless motivated to do so. It is the teacher's job to determine what will motivate his or her students to want to learn the materials at hand. Students won't invest their time or attention to things that are not of use.

I used to think students saying, "Why do I have to know this?" was an indictment on the quality of subject matter being taught. I now know this was a polite way of students telling me, "I don't care about this topic because you haven't explained to me why I should." It was my fault that they were unmotivated to learn. The onus was on me as their teacher to make sure that they could connect to the material in an authentic manner.

With that said, we need to not only make sure early in the lesson that students understand why learning is important and relevant in their lives, but cycle back to that purpose throughout the lesson.

Illustration. Once motivated to learn, students need clarity on what is being taught and what strategies, tools or methods can be used to accomplish the goal. Simply put, they need examples and plenty of them; however, effective use of examples is not a one-size-fits-all proposition. The type of exemplar used varies depending on the level of the learner.

Novice learners, or those not as familiar with a topic, need more concrete experience. Without necessary background experience, novice learners need to develop a basic understanding. Clarity here often comes in the form of vocabulary development and getting all students on the same page. To someone just learning to drive a car, oil is just black stuff you pour in the engine. Its meaning changes, however, as one becomes a more experienced driver, as should a teacher's use of examples.

This is one reason why sharing learning intentions and success criteria too early in a lesson can be futile. While it is true that making students aware of learning intentions and success criteria is a vital component of teacher clarity, it does not necessarily follow that this must occur at the beginning of each lesson. All too often, learners without experience on the topic cannot connect the learning to what they already know. Presenting information in such a fashion can cause frustration amongst students. When uninterested in the material, most tune out completely or persist out of compliance, not curiosity.

More advanced learners, on the other hand, already have background knowledge and a basis of understanding. They require more abstract illustrations and ones that will push their thinking. Concrete examples for the expert is counterproductive. Concrete, simple examples or strategies only lead to frustration and second-guessing. Knowing the level of each students dictates the form and function of the illustration.

Experimentation. All students need opportunities to learn and experiment. One way in which teachers can reduce ambiguity is by ensuring students have opportunities to process and play with the material. The best way for teachers to do this is to intentionally chunk their instructional content into small segments.

In his book, *Teaching with the Brain*, Eric Jenson (2005) provided guidelines for direct instruction:

- *Kindergarten through second grade students: 5 to 8 minutes;*
- *Third through fifth graders: 8 to 12 minutes; and*
- *Sixth through twelfth graders: 12-15 minutes.*

Many students have longer attention spans than the recommendations above, but our job as educators isn't just to get students to attend, it is to get them to learn. In order to learn, students need time to talk about, question, and play with material in order to best understand. Without enough mental or physical repetitions, students will never develop the neural pathways that are necessary to learn deeply.

When I learned to drive, my instructor taught me to always keep my hands at "9 and 3" on the steering wheel. He drilled into my head without my hands at this position, I would never be able to properly control where I go. I think the same can be said about our students. If we want students to safely get to their learning destination, we must also follow the "9 and 3" rule: every nine minutes of instruction/illustration our students need three minutes of experimentation. Intentionally stopping and allowing students time to process the information is a huge step at increasing clarity in the classroom.

Verification. Learners need verification of progress throughout learning. Verification comes in the form of feedback. Feedback throughout learning helps learners to know if what they are doing is correct and if they are on the right track. Without clear and consistent feedback, students struggle and question themselves. Teacher-student relationships are hampered by a lack of feedback during learning. When students don't receive frequent verification during learning, they question how much their teacher really cares.

Feedback is information used by the recipient to close the gap between what they know and where they need to go. Feedback comes in many different forms, but effective feedback has six characteristics:

1. ***Focused.*** Information is focused on the learning intention and not on the student. It is limited to the one thing students need to do to move forward.
2. ***Uplifting.*** Messages that encourage and provide a sense of hope that learning is within reach motivate students to achieve their goal and accomplish the task at hand. When students feel the goal is unreachable, they stop trying.
3. ***Edible.*** Feedback is phrased in student friendly language and presented in a non-threatening way based upon the unique needs of the learner.
4. ***Low Threat.*** Feedback that threatens a student's sense of self-efficacy will be ignored, walls will be put up, and understanding will be put to the side.
5. ***Enacted.*** The most important feedback is that which is utilized. Students must be provided opportunities to change their work. Too often, students are provided feedback and never given time to try and learn from their mistakes.
6. ***Descriptive.*** Feedback must be specific. It must describe a clear next step for the student.

Consistent use of effective feedback following these characteristics clears up student confusion and shows students their teacher cares about their success.

In the same way students need verification of their progress to enhance clarity, teachers must monitor their effectiveness as well. The best tool available for teachers to check for understanding and confusion in the classroom is formative assessment. Unfortunately, formative assessment has become one of the most over-used and misunderstood words in education. As with many other concepts in education, the term travels well, but the true understanding of the concept lags behind.

To change this, we should think of it as FOR-ME-TIVE assessment. Formative assessment is "for me" to adjust what I am doing rather than to determine what students are not doing.

Although many teachers have come to rely on exit slips and quick quizzes to gain insight on instructional needs, I have found the utilization of "Clarity Cards" to be more beneficial. One example of a Clarity Card can be made using a simple index card or half sheet of copy paper. On one side, students write one thing that they clearly understand from the lesson. On the opposite side, students share something that wasn't made clear or that they are still confused about from the lesson. This is an effective way for teachers to receive feedback on their instruction and has been proven over time to provide more insight to educators than traditional exit slips. A list of additional Clarity Card prompts can be found on the *www.significant72.com* website.

Feedback Intervention

In closing, the messages we send to students are in our words as well as our actions. Yeager et al. (2014) put this statement to the test to explore whether simple messages impact classroom success. After writing an essay on their hero, African American students of junior high age had their papers divided into two groups. In the first group, detailed and rigorous comments were added to the paper along with a brief note stating, "I'm giving you these comments so that you'll have feedback on your paper." On the papers of those in the second group, the message was altered slightly, along with the same type of detail and rigor commented upon, teachers added, "I'm giving you these comments because I have very high expectations and I know you can reach them."

The results indicated that 17 percent of students in the first group took the feedback and revised their work. Not too bad. But what about those who were told it was because the teacher cared? Amazingly, 71 percent of students who were told that their comments were made because of care chose to revise their essays. This is the message behind clarity. This is the message that courageous teachers communicate on a daily basis.

Reflect/Rethink/Refine

- *What is one way you get to know each child's STORY?*
- *To what extent will knowing your compass point change how you teach your students?*
- *Reflect on your current approach to providing feedback to students. How can you use the FUELED acronym to increase student clarity?*
- *Think of a lesson you taught and reflect on your clarity of motivation, illustration, experimentation, and verification?*
- *How might you work with colleagues to make your content and curriculum clearer for the students in your school?*

*Student Name:*____________________________________ *Date:*__________________

"My S.T.O.R.Y."

Instructions: Please answer the questions below in order to provide me with information on what you bring to our class and what I need to do to help you succeed.

***S**trengths*	My two greatest strengths in this subject area are…
***T**endencies*	I do my best work: ___working on my own ___working in a group ___meeting one-on-one ___working with a with the teacher ___working with a with the partner
***O**pportunities*	If you want me to get excited about learning, you should try…
***R**esources*	Someone I will turn to for help/ support during this class will be…
***Y**earnings*	I'd enjoy this class most if…

RAISE THE RELEVANCY

5 CHAPTER

Rachel overheard two students in the hallway talking about their siblings, recent college graduates who had just arrived home from Ireland after a month-long backpacking trip. As she listened, she couldn't help but reminiscence on her own experiences traveling overseas. Filled with these memories, she had an idea.

The next day, as her students entered their sixth-period European History, Rachel had a surprise planned for them. Reminding students of her travels and what she overheard outside the classroom, she explained that they would be going on an adventure of their own. They would be traveling to Europe. They had 5 minutes to pack their bags. "This is a 6-week journey," she told them, "You can only take what you can fit in your backpack. What will you bring?" Although several laughed at the idea, the students quickly got to work. After several minutes had passed, students shared with their cooperative groups what they would bring and why, with some adding to their lists as they listened to what others were bringing.

Moments later, Rachel called the students together and asked them to direct their attention to the large LCD panel at the front of the room. Using iMovie, she had created a movie trailer about backpacking through Europe. Included in the movie were pictures from her travels, as well as directions for the upcoming unit. Individually or in groups, students needed to choose a country to visit, explaining why it was chosen, come up with five historical "stops," and select two places that they wanted to visit for fun throughout the adventure. They then had to explain why those seven locales were important not only to that country's history, but to those citizens in the country. Further, they were told they would need to come up with a presentation, using a method of their choice, to convince their peers to take a similar trip and prove their learning to them. Excitedly, the students got to work, planning and preparing for their explorations.

When students find personal relevance and meaning in an activity, they work harder, perform better, persist longer, and are more intrinsically motivated to learn. When teachers purposefully design lessons based on student interest, and appeal to students' natural curiosities, they send students a message of respect: "I respect you too much to waste your time in my class. I am going to use what I know about you to connect my content in a way that enhances your love for learning."

Motivation?

The belief that students are not motivated to learn is prevalent in many schools. It is not uncommon to hear teachers discussing how inherently lazy and unmotivated today's children have become. Unfortunately, negativity begets negativity. Those negative attitudes and mindsets lead to unhealthy learning environments. Beyond that, such attitudes adversely affect both the teacher and the student. A vicious cycle of doom and gloom is set in motion. Rather than creating a sense of "wanting" to learn, students develop a sense of "having" to learn, which further exacerbates the problem.

In 2012, Nikhil Goyal, a 17-year-old high school student, wrote the book, *One Size Doesn't Fit All*. In the book, Goyal described his educational experience in a high performing high school. Goyal explained, "After being assimilated into the Syosset High School ecosystem, I noticed that I was bored as hell in class and absolutely nothing I was taught was relevant to real life. I was trained to be a drone. Outside of school, I was engaged with fascinating projects, having conversations with brilliant people, and enjoying life." He continued, "Testing, more homework and memorization did not quite equate to true learning" (Goyal, 2012). OUCH!

Is this really what students are thinking? Do others feel this way? If students at high-performing schools are thinking in this way, what must students with fewer educational opportunities be thinking?

To further understand the student perspective, YouthTruth looked at data they had gathered over a 5-year period based upon surveys they had administered to over 230,000 students in grades three through 12. The data, which were gathered through partnerships with schools in three dozen states, indicated that only 48 percent of secondary students felt what they learned in class would help them in real life. Diving deeper into the data, YouthTruth found that "high school students were slightly less likely than middle school students to feel that what they learned in class would help them outside of classroom. In other words, as students get closer to 'the real world,' they are even less likely to feel their learning in school is pertinent to their outside lives (*YouthTruth*, 2018).

WIIFM

Teachers like Rachel would not agree that today's learners lack motivation. They would argue that this generation of students may be more motivated than ever. It's just that what motivates 21st century learners is more likely to lay outside the classroom walls than within.

For decades, a child's need for connection, curiosity, knowledge acquisition, and peer interaction was only found at school. Learning in the classroom was the only game in town. This is no longer the case. Students can Google, YouTube, Instagram, and text at any moment in order to obtain information to fill those voids. Said another way, today's children tune into only one channel, *WIIFM: What's In It For Me.*

Courageous teachers don't lament for the good old days, when students "sat there respectfully and listened," or talk about how hard it is to motivate today's students. They embrace the fact that today's *iGEN* students want everything individualized, *Gamified, Entertaining,* and *Novel.* With that in mind, teachers like Rachel and the Significant Sallys of the world use the relationships they have established to creatively build learning experiences that meet these requirements. They capitalize on students' need for personal connection to information and others by making learning more relevant to students, their experiences, their communities, and their futures.

Yes, Motivation

Let's review what is known about motivation in academic settings, utilizing the Motivation Continuum below and drawing upon decades of research (Deci & Ryan, 2000; Vansteenkiste, Lens, & Ryan, 2006; Vansteenkiste et al., 2009). The concept of motivation is often simplified by educators into two broad categories, extrinsic or intrinsic. The simplification doesn't paint either a complete or clear picture of what drives student learning. Motivation is based upon the satisfaction of three basic psychological needs: autonomy, belongingness, and competence. The greater the degree with which these needs are fulfilled, the more intrinsic or autonomous one's motivation is, and the less controlled one feels.

Motivation Continuum					
No Motivation	**Controlled Motivation**		**Autonomous Motivation**		
Amotivation	**Extrinsic Motivation**				**Intrinsic Motivation**
			Internalized Motivation		
Unable and unwilling to find interest/ importance *passive *avoidant *oppositional	Coerced by external pressure *rewards/threats *punishments *need to please	Guided by internal feelings *must do or be *can't fail *need to save face *image, fame	Compelled by usefulness *importance *pertinence *advantageous	Encouraged by inherent value *inspired *hopeful *emboldened	Driven by interest *enjoyable *captivated *immersed
Insecure, afraid of failure, resistant to proceed	Tension, anxiety, decreased engagement and persistence	Feelings of guilt, shame, and decreased sense of self-worth	Sense of control, action out of free will, pleasure, energy, persistence, deeper learning, gratification, choice		
"Don't Have-to-vation"	"Have-to-vation"		"Want-to-vation"		

Degree to which basic needs of autonomy, belongingness, and competence are achieved →

Figure 5. Motivation continuum. Adapted with permission from Visser, Ket, Croiset, and Kusurkar (2017) and based upon work by Richard Ryan, Edward Deci, and Maarten Vansteenkiste.

"Have-to-vation"

"A recurring paradox in the contemporary K-12 classroom is that, although students educationally and developmentally benefit when teachers support their autonomy, teachers are often controlling during instruction" (Reeve, 2009, p. 159). Controlled motivation takes many forms, but it often leads to "have-to-vation" and external pressure from the student perspective. Whether it be the feeling they have to think, feel, or respond in a particular way; have to adapt to the teacher's perspective on an issue; or have to sit through lessons that are not relevant to their lives, learners feel inhibited. Frustration ensues as students go along to save-face and maintain perceived status, comply in order to get a grade or avoid punishment, or avoid the situation entirely by resisting the teacher's needs. All of these lead to lower student achievement, decreased participation, and dislike for learning.

"Want-to-vation"

According to self-determination theory, the more autonomy-supportive a learning environment, the higher the academic outcomes. Students who participate in schoolwork for completely intrinsic or internalized reasons are more involved and invested in learning, report higher levels of curiosity and enjoyment, and spend more time authentically engaged in learning. Further, autonomous motivation is associated with less maladaptive patterns of engagement including ignoring, anxiety, and boredom. Creating the conditions for students to "want to" learn more should be a priority of every courageous teacher.

Compliance Comes at a Cost

In addition to the negative academic outcomes mentioned above, students—like adults—find it very difficult to stay focused on things that they find boring. When they are disinterested in the content being taught, students must use their mental energies to pay attention, rather than to process information. The mental fatigue and cognitive inability to focus that follows undermines student feelings of connectedness to school and their teacher (Allensworth et al., 2018). The tension and anxiety created within students to try to persist through such a lesson causes many to misbehave and act out. The resulting classroom management issues negatively affect not only the individual's learning, but the learning of all students.

"Don't Have-to-vation"

Sadly, there are some students who appear to have little or no interest in being in school. This state, known as amotivation, is defined as the lack of desire or motive to act. These children appear to be lethargic, uninterested, and occasionally oppositional within the classroom. Students stuck in this motivational state are in need of someone to help them meet one or more of their basic psychological needs.

Although the assistance of a social worker or mental health clinician may be warranted, this shouldn't stop dedicated educators. Realizing that these students lack having their basic needs met, the courageous teacher seeks to develop relationships with the individual in order to create a sense of belonging and relatedness. No one is without motivation. Some students, however, have just not found theirs yet.

Again, Relationships Come First

As mentioned above, one of the substantive differences between the courageous teacher and comfortable teacher is that the courageous teacher leverages connections developed with students to cultivate personally relevant curriculum and instruction, as well as the autonomous behaviors that increase academic well-being.

The Rachels of the world take the time to get to know those in their classroom first as children and then as students. The daily investment and time they spend interacting with students in both formal and informal settings, better enables them to understand the desires, needs and assets each learner brings to the space. Utilization of these funds of knowledge to create more enriched learning experiences communicates both care and respect to a child. When students perceive that their teacher knows them both academically and personally, they are better positioned to take ownership of their learning (Edwards & Edick, 2013). Learning becomes the motivation for children in this classroom, as all three of their basic needs are being met.

This is in contrast to the comfortable teacher, who uses more extrinsic means to induce learning. The Dan the Drill Sergeants have a curriculum to teach and "hope" that students like what is being taught, but in the end, the students have no choice. They use coercion and bribes to engage students in lessons, using grades and external pressure as means of motivation. Putting all the responsibility on the learner makes outcomes more palatable for this type of teacher. They are not responsible for student investment; rather, unsuccessful students should have tried harder or paid closer attention.

The Chris the Camp Counselors also utilize controlling methods to motivate students; however, they control students much differently. They may know their students well, but rather than leverage those relationships to enhance learning, they have a tendency to use their relationships to entice students to partake in learning. Students are thus motivated by the need to please rather than the intrinsic value associated with the activity itself. Although this may produce short term results, this form of motivation is as troublesome as that utilized by the Dans. In this case, rather than pressure coming from the outside via carrots and sticks, motivation comes from the inside and the pursuit of acceptance.

Seeking a sense of self-worth by constantly looking for the approval of others is an exhausting endeavor. The guilt and shame associated when unable to live up to another's expectation impacts their self-confidence and self-esteem. Additionally, this form of motivation leads to more dependent and less independent learners.

This, in turn, creates students who are afraid to fail and lack the perseverance needed to succeed in school and life.

Further exacerbating this problem, many teachers who rely on controlling forms of motivation are teaching to themselves. They are often battling their own need for acceptance. The "disease to please," as coined by Harriet B. Braiker (2001), leads to the stress and anxiety of people at every age. Teachers who fall prey to this disorder can quickly soften curricular and instructional expectations when they see students struggling. Their emotional need to seek love and acceptance from their students overtakes their better judgment leaving teachers to feel guilt and shame themselves. More astute students pick up on these feelings, turn the tables on the teacher, and hold them emotionally hostage.

In my experience, autonomously motivated learners can only be developed by teachers who make relationship-building their first priority.

Bringing the Student to the Learning

Fundamentally, all teachers have certain content goals they must ensure students receive over the course of the year. Whether it be handed to them in a box or built off prioritized standards and created within professional learning communities, the curriculum taught to students in the classroom should depend upon the learners in that space. It is the teachers' job to find ways to bring their students to the curriculum.

Teachers who have a thorough understanding of their content standards, curricular goals, and assessment objectives, can set about developing effective instructional opportunities for their students. Such teachers are able to use what they know about student cultural backgrounds, prior experiences and levels of development to create authentic tasks that draw students into the curriculum. Keeping learning challenging yet interesting and meaningful not only reduces the monotony sometimes felt in school, but taps into student intrinsic motivation to learn.

This is where making learning relevant to students becomes so important. Relevance serves as a connector between the student's world and the content in order to deepen student learning and increase motivation to learn. When students find material personally meaningful and culturally relevant to their lives, they are able to become more authentically engaged in their education. This isn't just because of situational interest that has been triggered, but because they are able to access prior knowledge storage. Drawing upon what they already know about a topic lightens a student's cognitive load. Students can then allocate mental energy on tasks requiring higher levels of thought and concentration.

The story of Rachel's unit in the beginning of this chapter is an example of connecting the students to the curriculum by capturing their interest. Due to the relationships she had formed with her students, Rachel was able to learn about their interests in backpacking.

Knowing that many students in the affluent community she teaches, traveled overseas for vacation and backpacking trips, she was able to find a way to make learning about European history more interesting. This not only heightens initial interest, but provides learners an impetus for continued study. It is not uncommon to see students immerse themselves in very challenging tasks when they enjoy the topic. A goal of the teacher is to find materials that mimic that same level of engrossment.

Utilized well, relevancy serves to build off students' existing background knowledge, mental schemas and perspectives. It piques student curiosity and serves as a conduit between their worlds and the curriculum. But, minus those characteristics, relevancy can have no meaning at all.

Israel Scheffler (1969), an educational philosopher, once claimed, "Nothing is either relevant or irrelevant in and of itself. Relevant to what, how, and why?...That is the question" (p. 764). These words serve as a reminder to us that relevance varies depending on those questions. As an example, backpacking through Europe might not have caused the same level of excitement in a community where students don't commonly experience such trips. Students living in urban settings will find relevance in topics that students living in rural communities won't value at all. This is yet another reason that teachers must get to know their students well in order to teach them well.

Assessing students' initial interest in a topic is a great practice for teachers to determine how hard they will need to work to capture student interest. Researchers have consistently shown the interest level that students have in taking a class is a great predictor of how interested they will stay throughout the class. Conversely, those with low levels of interest need to be shown the relevance that the class has to their personal journey.

One way teachers can gauge interest level is by asking students to rate their interest on a topic/unit on a scale of 1 to 5 and explain their rationale for giving it such a score. Using this as formative information, teachers can establish how hard they will need to work to bring the student to the learning.

Bring the Learning to the Student

Once students have become captivated by a topic, it is important for teachers to sustain the level of interest throughout the unit of study. Students who see the continued value of their learning experience greater involvement, more positive task attitudes, and greater connection to the subject matter. Further, students involved in meaningful academic experiences including being asked interesting questions, digging deeper in a topic for deeper understanding, applying the subject to problems in life outside of school and then discussing ideas with teachers and peers, are consistently more engaged and experience higher levels of social and academic outcomes (Marks, 2000).

Carl Wieman, Nobel Prize Winner of Physics and professor at Stanford, recommended that students be provided with intentional and explicit opportunities to discuss why each topic is worth learning, how it operates in the real world, why it makes sense, and how it connects to things the student already knows (Rabinovitz, 2013). Teaches can afford students the opportunity to answer these questions by creating a four-quadrant Frayer model chart or utilize the "What's In It For Me" worksheet found on the www.significant72.com website. The worksheet asks students to individually answer the following four questions:

1. *How does this topic connect to what we already know?*
2. *Why is this topic worth learning?*
3. *How would you define this topic?*
4. *Where might we see an example of this in the real world?*

Upon completion, the worksheet can be shared with fellow students or collected by the teacher to see the connections students are constructing.

Activities such as the one mentioned above are particularly helpful for students who have lower expectations for the course. Hulleman and Harackiewicz (2009) tried a similar activity as a relevance intervention with high school science students. Students were asked to write a one-paragraph essay that applied the lesson to their life or to the life of someone they knew. The students who took part in the intervention scored higher than expected on end-of-course assessments and reported more interest in science. Similar studies have produced comparable results, indicating that this practice may be beneficial at all levels.

Not only does raising the relevance in lessons develop student intrinsic motivation to learn, but it enhances academic outcomes and develops stronger relationships among those in the classroom.

Driving Their Own Learning

Although providing students with experiences that connect learning to their lives is a proven way to develop more autonomously motivated learners, teachers can more quickly intrinsically motivate students by setting time aside for personal exploration. Allowing students opportunities to fully research and investigate topics of their choosing is a guaranteed way to see intrinsic motivation in action.

Project-Based Learning

One of the challenges many teachers face when trying to develop intrinsic motivation is not deeply understanding what is needed for students to be successful when given more independent opportunities. Without having a firm grasp on how motivation develops via the motivational continuum, many educators fall prey to the "voice and choice" mantra and give students free choice to explore.

The failure to realize students must feel a sense of autonomy, belonging and competence, in order to experience intrinsic motivation, creates student frustration. Learning is lost and time is wasted.

True project-based learning, often referred to as PBL, like that advocated by The Buck Institute for Education, utilizes standards-based content to develop important critical thinking skills. PBL is a rigorous process that calls on students to solve meaningful problems by asking questions, finding resources, setting personal learning goals, and using a variety of metacognitive skills, while reflecting on the inquiry process throughout.

Although this process does have elements of voice and choice, it provides students with the support, structure, and collaborative opportunities needed to not only stay engaged over time, but also transfer skills developed into other areas of school and life.

Genius Hour

Many teachers have found the value of implementing Genius Hour time into their instructional day in order to allow students to explore their individual passions. Genius Hour entails providing students anywhere from a period or two per week to work on an inquiry-based project of their choosing. Students generate a list of "wonders" around the topic, either subject-based or open-ended, then set about investigating, researching, and experimenting hypotheses. Students then determine a method of sharing their findings with classmates and peers. Teachers are integral in the success of such projects as they are conferring with and probing thinking throughout the journey.

A few years ago, Paul Solarz was introducing Passion Time to his fifth graders and helping them brainstorm ideas that they might want to explore throughout the year. Many children were rapidly scribbling down ideas, while a few looked like they were struggling a bit. When he approached one student, he noticed a tear in the child's eye and the look of fear in the child's face. Paul asked him why he was so upset, and he told Paul he had no passions and that he'd never be able to do a Genius Hour project.

Paul had an idea. He asked his classroom assistant to watch the class while he and the student went for a walk. "Who was your fourth grade teacher last year?" he asked. "We're going to visit her!" Off they went.

When they got to her room, Paul asked, "What do you think would be a good topic for our friend to do a genius hour project on?"

The teacher replied, "Oh, I bet he'd love to teach other kids how to use GoAnimate! He was super excited about it last year!"

The expression on the child's face after he heard his previous year's teacher's suggestion was priceless. He became excited to get started on making a video teaching other children how to make an animation using the GoAnimate website. He spent the next 10 class periods researching all of the features the site had to offer and made an 18-minute instructional video to show what he learned.

His final reflection read, "Thanks to the video and the help of my two teachers, I learned how to teach others GoAnimate and how to use a quick time player. And, it was so much fun too!"

Design Thinking

While Genius Hour is often a more student-centered exploration, Design Thinking is a more human-centered approach. Made popular by Stanford University and companies like IDEO, Design Thinking involves students working together to solve real-world problems that affect others in the school or community. The process begins with empathy, as students interview others in order to better understand their needs and to begin generating potential solutions. The development of empathy in this way is not only particularly beneficial for developing a sense of purpose within students but fosters the social-emotional skills students, need to be successful in all walks of life.

Laura McBain, director of the K12 lab in Stanford University's d.school, stated that this program *"allows students to think about the challenges the world is facing and puts them in the driver's seat to be really engaged to solve problems, to feel empowered, and to change the world!"*

Relevance Leads to Action

Students engage when they have relationships with teachers who know their content and who make sure learning is relevant, interesting, and challenging (Fisher, Frey, Quaglia, Smith, & Lande, 2017). When used well, relevancy captures interest, ignites a need to know more, fuels students to delve deeper into their learning, and drives them to want to continue their learning outside the schoolhouse doors. Students who can't wait to run home to learn more are the epitome of autonomous motivation and proof that a teacher has made a difference.

Reflect/Rethink/Refine

- *How does your teaching improve when you are more autonomously motivated?*
- *In what ways does "have-to-vation" impact learning?*
- *How might you make your lessons more relevant to student lives outside the classroom?*
- *How can you provide opportunities for students to drive their own learning?*
- *In what ways can your school better meet the needs of today's iGEN students?*

ACCELERATE ACHIEVEMENT 6 CHAPTER

Maddie's Message:
I know I matter when my teacher helps me feel successful.

Two weeks into the semester, it finally happened! Students were beginning to believe in themselves and their math abilities. It didn't come easy, but when it did, it was like a landslide of positivity swept across the hearts and minds of Mr. Wolf's class of eighth graders.

Michelle, with butterflies in her stomach, nervously walked up to Mr. Wolf as he worked with a small group. "Mr. Wolf, is this right?" she asked. As he turned to review her work, he noticed others in the class look over, almost as if her work represented the efforts of everyone. He looked over her paper.

"Yeah! That's it!" he said excitedly. "Class. Stop what you are doing. Please look up here. Michelle has figured out problem two. I want her to explain to everyone how she did it."

Michelle, proud of her accomplishment, eagerly explained the strategy she used to solve the challenging problem to her peers. She walked the others, step-by-step, through her thinking process, what she had done to get the answer, and how she kept writing the equation incorrectly. Then, by relying on a different method, she was able to come to the correct solution.

While Mr. Wolf thanked Michelle for sharing with the class and recognized her perseverance in front of the group, Tarah, a friend of Michelle's, began to smile. Sure, she was happy that Michelle had finally cracked the code, but more importantly, she had a renewed confidence in her own abilities. "If Michelle can do it, I can do it!" she thought inside.

Little did Mr. Wolf know that the feelings that Tarah had were shared by many other students. Michelle's breakthrough signaled a breakthrough for the group as a whole. It was evident that every student's confidence had been altered by Michelle's results. Suddenly, everyone was experiencing success in his classroom. The enthusiasm was truly contagious.

When students reach that point when they see their efforts are producing the results they desire, they are recognized for their growth by significant others, and the sensations associated with feeling competent take over their body, they believe they can do anything. They are ready to take on the world. If peers in similar situations are witness to the event, they want a taste of it as well. Success leads to success!

Creating the Conditions for Success

Albert Einstein once said, "I never teach my pupils. I only attempt to provide the conditions in which they can learn." The minds of most educators are immediately filled with thoughts of beautiful classrooms, well-planned and executed lessons, and highly engaged students when reading this quote. While it is natural to read those words and think about the external environments needed to produce student success, courageous teachers think first about creating the "internal" conditions needed for students to thrive.

After a decade of teaching, I thought I had the formula for student success figured out. GC + GI + GA = SS. In other words, Great Curriculum plus Great Instruction plus Great Assessment equals Successful Students. Easy. But wrong! I then tried a new formula. BC + BI + BA = SS. Or, Better Curriculum plus Better Instruction plus Better Assessment equals Successful Students. Wrong again!

Like Michelle, in the introduction for this chapter, I didn't give up. I began seeing the problem in a different way, realizing that it was much more than I originally thought. After years, I finally stumbled on the correct formula. (GC + GI + GA) SE = ISS. That is, the sum of Great Curriculum plus Great Instruction plus Great Assessment times Self Efficacy equals Incredibly Successful Students. Even better!

Self-Efficacy

One of the primary purposes for developing significant relationships in the classroom is to increase a child's sense of self-efficacy. Self-efficacy describes the belief one has in their ability to meet challenges and complete tasks successfully. Students can have the content knowledge and conceptual skills to achieve, but if they don't have the faith in their own abilities to successfully demonstrate what they can do, they will not experience success. Believing that one can be successful is a prerequisite to putting forth sustained effort (Farrington et al., 2012). Self-efficacy affects how students feel, think, and behave.

Self-efficacy is a strong indicator of students' motivation and learning. Students' belief in their ability to learn and perform well in school can predict their level of academic performance above and beyond their measured level of ability and prior performance (Dweck et al., 2014). Students with high levels of self-efficacy are more willing to set challenging goals, undertake and persist with difficult assignments, and solve complex problems than their peers with similar ability yet lower self-efficacy (Pajares & Urdan, 2006). Self-efficacy has also been proven to increase student use of self-regulatory processes such as goal setting, self-monitoring, self-assessment and strategy use. Further, a positive sense of self-efficacy influences students emotionally, decreasing their levels of stress and anxiety while increasing their feelings of excitement and positive arousal (Zimmerman, 2000).

Although many might equate self-efficacy to self-confidence, the two are quite different. While self-confidence relates to how likely one feels they are to succeed in general, self-efficacy is more task/subject specific and very situation dependent. It is a belief in one's ability to succeed in a particular situation. A student who has high levels of self-efficacy can be self-confident; however, a student who has low levels of self-confidence cannot also be high in self-efficacy. Confidence has a positive effect on one's self-efficacy, but the opposite is not true. Students who feel capable of performing at high levels and excelling in school expect—and almost always achieve—proportionate outcomes.

Perception Versus Reality

Cognitive psychologist Albert Bandura (1977) indicated when self-efficacy is lacking, people will be ineffective, even if they know what to do. The reality is that students like Tarah, in the illustration to start the chapter, may have the knowledge and skills to tackle the challenging problems presented to them by Mr. Wolf, but, if they don't believe they can do the more thought-provoking work, they are unable to perform. Student perceptions of their abilities aren't necessarily accurate. As educators, we must work diligently to change those perceptions. Bandura suggested that self-efficacy is developed and fueled through four sources: mastery experiences, vicarious learning, social persuasion, and physical/emotional state.

Mastery Experiences. Past success is a huge determinant of future success. When students confront challenges similar to ones in which they have previously succeeded, they believe that they can succeed again. Students rely on mastery experiences from their past when encountering new obstacles. Knowing they have succeeded develops the belief that they will again. Trusting they have the capabilities to be successful increases their self-efficacy and tendency to remain resilient and perseverant. In contrast, when unsuccessful at a task, self-efficacy is lowered, and students become worried they won't be successful the next time around. Failure undermines self-efficacy, especially for students with fixed mindsets (Pajares & Urdan, 2006). Success pulls students towards more difficult work, whereas failure pushes them away.

Vicarious Learning. The second most powerful source for self-efficacy is vicarious learning. Children constantly learn from watching others, not only inside, but outside the classroom. Students who see a peer, or someone similar to themselves in some way, triumph they begin to believe the goal is attainable for them as well.

Observing others perform and be reinforced for doing a similar task is powerful. Hearing Michelle explain how she tackled the difficult math problem gave Tarah the belief that she, too, could come up with the correct solution also; "If someone like me can do it, so can I." The opposite, however, is equally as important for teachers to remember. When students see classmates struggle, they are more likely to perceive they will struggle. This can cause a child to question their own abilities; again, self-efficacy works both ways, and can have a self-fulfilling prophecy effect.

Social Persuasion. Social persuasion, the third source of self-efficacy, refers to the feedback provided to students by credible and trustworthy sources like teachers or friends. Probably the most commonly used among the four, social persuasion is the one source that has the most potential to negatively impact a student's sense of efficacy. The messages that students receive from their loved and respected ones carry weight and have meaning.

Teachers must be very cognizant of the feedback they provide. It is easier to weaken student self-efficacy than raise through encouragement. Negative feedback, especially of the more person-centered variety, becomes a student's self-talk. It is like that last song one hears on the radio in the morning before they walk into school; it plays over and over again through their head, all day long. The words teachers use replay time after time in student's minds. Educators must ask themselves which tune they want on repeat in each child's head—a negative one or an uplifting one?

In my junior year in high school, after a long, hard basketball practice, Coach Hale, our varsity basketball coach, pulled me aside. Sitting down next to me on the bleachers, he put his arm around me, looked me eye-to-eye, and said, "Greg Wolcott. You know, God doesn't give normal people names like that. He only gives people names like that who are going to do great things in their lives. They are going to help others, inspire others, and make a difference in this world. I want you to know I believe in Greg Wolcott." Wow! I was blown away. But what is most important to know is the impact those words had on me. Not only did they propel me to a season high in points, but more importantly those words have held a prominent place in my head and my heart. Since that day, anytime I have felt down, lacked confidence or doubted myself, I have heard Coach Hale's voice and his words in my head. All teachers should strive to provide such positive words of encourage for their students.

Physical/Emotional State. The final source of self-efficacy comes from one's physiological and emotional state. Overlooked at times, one's physiological and affective state plays a critical role in performance. Students' levels of stress, anxiety, energy, and enthusiasm impact how successful they feel they will perform in school.

Bodily reactions and emotional arousals such as nervousness, sweating, and faster heart rates act as signals to students that they lack the competence to successfully perform the task, which thus lowers their self-efficacy (Hattie & Alderman, 2013, p. 65).

Lyubomirsky et al. (2005) found that the more positive emotions an individual experience, the more likely they are to succeed in their workplace, receive higher evaluations from teachers or supervisors, and the more benefit they bring to the workplace or classroom. Students' positive emotions trickle to other students, and their teachers, generating more enthusiasm by all. This is not only a win for the individual student, but for all students.

Quick Wins

Henry Ford once stated, "Whether you think you can or think you can't, you are right." Given the importance of enhancing a child's self-efficacy beliefs, courageous teachers intentionally create opportunities for all students to experience success. They do this in part, because they want students to feel good about themselves, but also because they know they cannot press students to succeed without first building their sense of success within a subject area.

Teachers must strive to provide students with quick wins early in each course. Quick wins help students not only feel their efforts are leading them in the right direction, but that they are developing the knowledge and capabilities to handle tasks and challenges thrown at them. Initial success increases the likelihood of subsequent success (Iso-Ahola & Dotson, 2016). Daily wins provide a needed jump start to each child's success, and lead to students feeling that they can succeed in the course.

Rather than focus on end of the unit outcomes and asking students to constantly measure themselves against the finish line or, more often than not, wonder until the final exam how they are doing, courageous teachers provide opportunities for immediate success. They specifically schedule recognition points into the course framework, ensuring there are opportunities for students to show mastery of material, and get recognized for their progress. Mastery moments where students can shine in the success builds psychological momentum.

Meghan, a high school chemistry teacher, changed her practices to help students view themselves as successful learners. Having once waited until the fourth week of the semester to assess students on the entire periodic table, she broke her assessment into smaller components. At the end of each week, she tested students on their knowledge of a reduced number of the chemical elements and the properties of each. Breaking the big assessment down into smaller pieces, while at the same time keeping the difficulty level high, allowed Meghan to push her students a little further while developing beliefs in their abilities.

Winning Streaks

Although quick wins are important for all students, they are not enough for those who don't typically experience success. Students who frequently succeed can have a minor setback and not fail to lose momentum. They can brush off defeat and move forward. Students who do not typically achieve as much, however, will often write off the isolated triumph as luck. They need to repeatedly experience a sense of accomplishment to begin developing an "I can do this!" mindset. They need to stack victories in order to believe they are capable. If not, they are likely to slide into an "I can't" view of themselves, leading to a lack of perseverance and a belief that the outcome of the course is already decided. Success leads to further success, and failure leads to further failure (Iso-Ahola & Dotson, 2016).

Goal Setting

Goal setting is an important cognitive process that impacts student motivation and increases self-efficacy. An excellent form of goal setting, developed by NYU professors Gabriele Oettingen and Peter Gollwitzer, is the WOOP strategy. Based on over 20 years of research, WOOP (Wish, Outcome, Obstacle, Plan) relies heavily on the concept of mental-contrasting. Whereas traditional SMART (Specific, Measurable, Achievable, Relevant, and Time-bound) goals are beneficial in some ways, students have a tendency to become fixated on their outcome, giving up the minute a challenge arises or when the goal seems unattainable. This often happens because barriers to accomplish were never thought out ahead of time. Mental contrasting forces students to think about and identify potential obstacles along the way and identify a plan for overcoming those hurdles when confronted. Process-oriented goal setting methods, like WOOP, not only help engrained a growth mindset in students but help develop perseverance as well.

- **Wish.** I want to become a better writer.
- **Outcome.** I will get me story published in the Young Authors contest.
- **Obstacle.** I sometimes let feedback slow my progress.
- **Plan.** If feedback slows my progress, then I will remind myself that mistakes are okay and proof I am trying.

Further information on WOOP goal development, including additional examples, can be found at www.characterlab.org.

Whether it be SMART goals or WOOP goals, one size doesn't fit all situations. Teachers should base both the length of the goal and the frequency students check in on their progress on the age of the student and need of the learner. Younger students, or students who need to feel a sense of competence more often in order to stay motivated, should set short-term goals and check on their progress more frequent than older students, who are able to maintain focus longer.

Grade Range	Length of Goals	Frequency Checks
Kindergarten - Second Grade	2 weeks	Every 1-2 days
Third Grade - Fifth Grade	4 weeks	Every week
Sixth - Eighth Grade	8 weeks	Every 2 weeks
Ninth - Twelfth Grade	12 weeks	Every 4 weeks

Figure 6. Goal setting guidelines.

Recognition Rituals

For some kids, every day in school is a talent show; for others, they never get a day to ever show their talents. With this in mind, teachers should have recognition rituals, or regularly scheduled opportunities for all students to share their successes. Such rituals fuel all four sources of self-efficacy. They celebrate success and enforce mastery experiences for the student being recognized. They serve as vicarious learning opportunities for peers. They serve as feedback opportunities for students to receive feedback and words of encouragement from both teachers and peers/respected others. Finally, they create positive emotions amongst everyone in the classroom.

Elizabeth, a fifth-grade teacher in Arizona, and also a die-hard Chicago Cubs fan, started a daily win board in her classroom. On a bulletin board in the back of her room, she placed a replica of the big "W" flag Cubs fans fly when they win a game. Then every day, she asked students to write their daily win on a post-it note and tack it to the bulletin board next to the flag. Not only did this provide students in her class with an opportunity to share a success, but students frequently stopped and read one another's postings.

Figure 7. Weekly Win Picture.

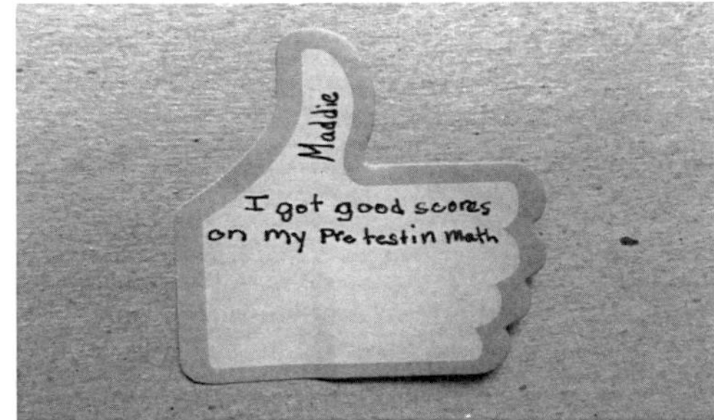

Figure 7. Weekly Win Picture.

Praise Plans

In his book, Big Potential, New York Times bestselling author Shawn Achor *(2018) stated:* "What so many fail to recognize is that praise is actually a renewable resource. Praise creates a Virtuous Cycle- the more you give, the more you enhance your own supply.

When done right, praise primes the brain for higher performance, which means the more we praise, the more success we create. And the more successes there are, the more there is to praise" (p. 117).

I experienced this firsthand with an experiment that I asked my graduate students to undertake for a 16-week action research class that I taught. After surveying students in their classes on sense of belonging, teacher-student relationships, and developing an academic achievement baseline, each student was given 45 cents in the form of five nickels and 20 pennies. They were then asked to try and "spend" the 45 cents each day. Five times during the day, they would stop, make eye-contact with the student, give a high five, and highlight something they did right, such as, "Leslie, your writing is awesome. You described the setting so well, I felt like I was there in person." They would keep track of how they were doing by moving a nickel from the right pocket to the left after each interaction. Then, 20 times each day, they would recognize student accomplishment with verbal praise. Verbal praise started again with eye-contact, but was much simpler in nature, such as, "Curtis, nice effort!" This time, teachers were asked to move a penny from pocket to pocket.

After 3 weeks, the results of the experiment were tallied. Not only did students show huge growth academically during the short duration of the intervention, but the survey results of both teacher-student relationships and sense of belonging with peers more than doubled. One surprise finding, however, was that even though boys were praised almost twice as much as girls, the girls' survey results grew at a higher rate than boys. Focus groups were conducted with the girls to try and learn why their results were higher despite receiving "less" praise. Interestingly, the girls pointed out, that even though they didn't personally receive the praise, just having more praise in the classroom made it a better place to learn and a "more fun place to be."

Although this research my students and I conducted was very informal in nature, I believe it is an excellent example of the "virtuous cycle" in action.

Social-Emotional Learning

In recent years, educators around the world are starting to understand the importance of developing students' social emotional learning skills. Learning how physical and emotional states affect how people feel, think, and act is critical to the development of self-efficacious learners.

Two ideas from the world of positive psychology are particularly helpful when discussing this topic. The first, developed by famed researcher Barbara Fredrickson (2001), is a theory known as "broaden and build." Fredrickson found that positive states expand people's thinking, as well as their intellectual, physical and social resources. These resources increase a person's resilience and fill them with a sense of optimism and hope.

In this state the filters are off and the possibilities seem endless, allowing us to take in great amounts of information. Students in this condition are more attentive, more curious, more resilient and more open to tackling challenges. On the flip side, consistent negative emotions, funnel people into "downward cycles" which often lead to a focus on the negative. When emotions are negative, learners take in less information, as the brain begins scanning the environment for threats. This natural reaction to stress and anxiety, which has evolved over thousands of years, is actually a protective mechanism used to keep us from danger. Students in this state shut off the outside world and can focus on everything except learning. Educators must provide students with strategies and tools to combat these natural reactions brought upon by their negative emotions.

In order to assist students in dealing with this downward state, educators can teach students a three-step process to improve student self-regulation. The Recognize-Categorize-Strategize model is the foundational process needed to improve social emotional learning within both students and adults. The three interdependent phases not only help students slow down and process information, but begin productively putting strategies in place to think more positively.

This process begins with student self-awareness, or recognizing the physical sensations going on within their bodies. Noticing such feedback that the body is providing is a key first step. Using Michelle from the introduction as an example, would look like this, "I have butterflies in my stomach and my heart seems to be speeding up." Students then are taught to categorize their emotions. Categorizing the emotion helps students make sense of it, and is a form of self-compassion. An example would be Michelle saying, "I am feeling stress." It is important not to think of stress as good or bad, but to view it simply as information. If taught proactive ways to deal with stress from her teacher and other school staff, Michelle can then draw upon strategies to strategize her feelings. This final component develops a child's self-management skills. A complete cycle would sound like, "I recognize I have butterflies in my stomach and my heart seems to be speeding up. I am feeling stress. I will do some deep belly breaths to slow my heart down, so I can go up to the teacher and share my math paper."

Concepts like "broaden and build" and Recognize, Categorize, Strategize are critically important for both teachers and students to understand. It is only with an understanding of these topics that one is truly able to gain control of one's physical and emotional states.

(GC + GI + GA) SE = ISS

Developing self-efficacy by accelerating success in the classroom has strong psychological effects on students, impacting their thoughts, feelings and actions. As has been shown repeatedly in this chapter, self-efficacy is a force multiplier, in that student belief in their own abilities greatly affects how successful they will become.

When students believe they are likely to succeed in meeting academic demands in a classroom, they are much more likely to try hard and to persevere in completing academic tasks, even if they find the work challenging or do not experience immediate success (Farrington et al., 2012). Regardless of the curriculum, instruction, or assessment used within the classroom, if students do not believe, they will never achieve. Students with high levels of self-efficacy believe that anything is possible, while students without it believe that nothing is possible.

Reflect/Rethink/Refine

- *Why is increasing self-efficacy so important to student success?*
- *In what ways can you help students in your class get on winning streaks?*
- *How do you recognize student success in the classroom?*
- *How can you work with your colleagues to improve your collective teacher efficacy?*
- *Write a WOOP Goal for increasing student self-efficacy and share with a colleague.*

GUARANTEE SUPPORT

7 CHAPTER

Maddie's Message:
I know I matter when I am supported by my teachers and classmates.

The day was about to begin at Scott Middle School. The loudspeaker came on as the principal announced, "Just a reminder, today is STAR 7." This had little meaning to students, but staff knew this meant they would be taking time out of their seventh period class for intentional relationship-building activities.

After attending a presentation over the summer, members of the leadership team decided to implement Significant 72. This concept, originating in Woodridge School District 68, a preschool through eighth grade district in the western suburbs of Chicago, calls for teachers to intentionally set aside time to form strong and caring relationships with and between students. This is done by allocating the first 3 days of the school year (72 hours), as well as time after long weekends and holiday breaks, to building connections. By specifically focusing on developing caring communities in classrooms, students not only feel cared for by their teachers, but by their classmates too.

Understanding the importance of relationship development in the teen and preteen years made Significant 72 a natural fit for the building. And, it didn't take long for staff to not only see but feel the benefits as well. By winter break, the staff was hooked, and by the end of the year, they couldn't help but think of ways to take it to the next level. The ripple effects created from the intense focus on relationship development were felt across the school. In their first year, office discipline referrals decreased by one third, minor classroom disciplinary infractions dropped by over 50 percent, academic growth was noted on the state accountability measurement in both reading and math, and the overall climate in the building was more positive. Relationship-building went from something they did, to who they were as educators.

The next fall, staff at Scott took relationship development even more seriously. Building off momentum created in year one, they started a school initiative called, "STAR 72: Students Teachers Accelerating Relationships." The staff decided that in addition to what was done the first year, one period each day throughout the year would be set aside for Significant 72. From the seven periods a day, the staff created a rotating schedule to ensure one-period each day would be focused on relationship-building.

They started with a blank calendar and after the first three days of school, numbered days one to seven and then repeated the cycle throughout the year, skipping only holidays and days with which they expected all staff to conduct relationship-building activities. STAR 1 indicated to staff that first period teachers would conduct whole-class relationship-building activities. STAR 2 meant that second period teachers would conduct such activities, and so forth. By rotating days in such a manner, staff were assured that students would spend 15 minutes each day intentionally connecting with their teachers and peers.

The second part of the school improvement plan brought into play the "two" in "STAR 72." In addition to whole group activities every seventh day, teachers were asked to schedule small group relationship-building activities at least 2 days per week. These quick activities, lasting anywhere from 3 to 5 minutes, would help develop bonds among small groups of students and enhance cooperative learning throughout the building. The majority of teachers, after seeing the results of the small group exercises, began incorporating them into daily lessons. Staff noticed that these activities gave them deeper insight into the students who sat in front of them, allowing them to better tailor instruction to meet individual needs. The exercises were also enhancing peer relationships and fostering an even strong atmosphere of trust and acceptance throughout the building.

Scott Middle School is just one of over 300 schools across the globe who have made teacher-student relationship-building a top priority. Placing connections before curriculum is "the" priority standard that must be taught in schools today. Significant 72 teachers understand that without connections, curriculum has no meaning. The relationships between the teachers and students, and between students with one another, bring the content to life. And, as I have emphasized throughout this book, when relationships nourish, students flourish.

Psychological Safety

In the complex, ever-changing educational ecosystem known as the modern-day classroom, students must be guaranteed support from both their teachers and their peers. Although developing exceptionally strong relationships with and between students is an excellent outcome in itself, there are other benefits of such bonds, namely the psychological safe environment that is produced. It is only when such conditions are fostered that students have a chance to reach their fullest potential.

Google It

As part of their continual improvement efforts, Google set out to learn what the best teams within their organization did that made them "effective." *Project Aristotle* was the code-name for the 2-year study that gathered both qualitative and quantitative data from over 180 teams.

Once gathered, more than 250 attributes were tabulated and analyzed in hopes of learning what was needed to make the perfect team. When all was said and done, the results were somewhat surprising. Who was on the team mattered much less than how team members interacted, structured their daily work, and viewed their contributions to Google's mission.

According to the re:Work report on *Project Aristotle*, five key characteristics were identified amongst the most "effective" teams:

Psychological Safety: Feeling safe to take risks and be vulnerable among peers.
Dependability: The act of being accountable and getting things done.
Structure and Clarity: Team members' understanding of expectations and the process of fulfilling those expectations.
Meaning: Finding a sense of purpose in the work (i.e., personal importance).
Impact: Belief that one's work is valued and is making a difference.

Although each of these features enhanced team success, the impact of one particular attribute outweighed all of the others. Google learned that psychological safety was the most important component because it provided a foundation upon which the other four could be built. Without psychological safety, none of the other characteristics were possible. Paul Santagata, Google's Head of Industry, explained, "There's no team without trust."

When taking a deeper dive into Google's findings, educators will see obvious parallels with successful teams. Greatness in the classroom, like the workplace, is dependent on trust. When members of the team feel safe in the group, they are more willing to give their perspective, ask questions, and provide feedback to one another. Feeling free to take risks and make mistakes, knowing that one will not be made fun of by peers or punished by a superior, has a broader effect, which increases motivation and leads to higher levels of engagement. In contrast, ridicule causes funneling and focusing, leads to insecurity and embarrassment, decreases participation, and deteriorates any semblance of trust which has been created.

Engagement in the Classroom

If 1 million U.S. students were polled and asked about their level of engagement in school based on their school environment, relationships with adults, and whether or not they felt valued at school, what would they say? According to Gallup, who conducted such a survey, the answer depends on the age of the student. The results from their 2015 student poll showed that student engagement decreased from a high of 75% in fifth grade to 32% in 11th grade, then raised slightly up to 34% in 12th grade. If that wasn't sobering enough information, 10% of students surveyed were classified as both disengaged and discouraged. How does this happen?

One reason engagement may be lacking in schools today is the lack of a common description and full understanding of what engagement means. Without this knowledge, many teachers create compliance-based environments within the classroom which do not provide the psychological safety that students need to be successful.

Engagement: What It Is

Engagement describes the extent to which a student is actively involved in a learning activity (Wellborn, 1991). Four types of engagement can be found in the classroom: behavioral engagement, emotional engagement, cognitive engagement, and agentic engagement. Three of these four types are initiated by the teacher, and one—agentic engagement—is initiated by the student. Let's take a closer look at each:

- ***Behavioral Engagement.*** Students are behaviorally engaged in the classroom when they are on-task, following the rules of the room, paying attention, and participating (at the direction of the teacher) in what is being taught.

- ***Emotional Engagement.*** Emotional engagement refers to student interest, curiosity, enthusiasm and feelings (positive of negative) for what is being taught.

- ***Cognitive Engagement.*** Children who are thinking deeply about a topic, connecting it to the world, problem-solving, or strategically thinking are cognitively engaged. "Brain sweat" is a sign of cognitive engagement.

- ***Agentic Engagement.*** Agentic engagement refers to students' constructive contribution into the flow of the lesson they receive (Reeve & Tseng, 2011). This occurs when students are actively initiating learning by offering input, asking questions, communicating their thoughts without solicitation, seeking clarification, seeking ways to add personal relevance to the lesson, or requesting assistance such as modeling or feedback from the teacher. They are proactively trying to personalize and enrich what is learned and the circumstances in which they have learned (Reeve & Tseng, 2011). Students who are agents of their own learning are no longer just receiving classroom instruction from their teacher; they are drivers of their own learning.

With a more thorough understanding of engagement comes a deeper appreciation for the importance of relationship development in the classroom. It is obvious that strong teacher-student relationships enhance all four types of engagement, but agentic engagement, in many aspects the gold standard, can only be achieved within the confines of a psychologically safe environment. Psychological safety, in turn, cannot occur unless students feel they can be vulnerable in front of their peers. With this thought in mind, there is a need for educators to place intentional emphasis on providing students the support they need to take risks, open themselves up for feedback, and not fear that their actions will lead to embarrassment or peer ridicule.

Support: Noun or Verb?

The word *support* is both a noun and a verb. The word is most often seen in education as a noun, in that teachers are ready to provide students "emotional or practical help" after they struggle. Most teachers are very good at this part of their job. Every teacher has a bag of tricks or stack of potential interventions to provide when students begin to fail; however, this isn't the support that students need most. Herein lies the problem in many classrooms.

Providing support after struggle is a "wait to fail" mentality that conceals a flawed mindset. That is, stumbles are not good and need to be fixed. This thought pattern, although subconscious in nature, is made visual throughout the day in how educators act and respond to students. Children pick up on this and become cautious in what they do and how they act, hoping they won't need support. These students then have a tendency to avoid struggle and failure at all costs, never wanting to be wrong or dare admit to being wrong. Their fear of failure limits their use of effective strategies that could help them succeed. This creates fixed mindsets and performance avoidance behaviors within students, both of which lead to decreased self-efficacy, engagement, and help-seeking, as well as increased test anxiety, stress, and worry.

Viewing support as a verb, as in "to give encouragement and approval to someone because you want the person to succeed," changes those outcomes. In this way, teachers provide support so that students can struggle in a safe place where mistakes are okay and tackling challenges is a natural part of the learning journey. In these classrooms, students consistently strive to get better, learn more, and grow. Students who are encouraged to venture out of their comfort zone, knowing someone has their back, have proven to be more perseverant, demonstrate a preference for challenging tasks, adopt deep learning strategies, have better self-regulation and long-term retention, and are more intrinsically motivated (Edwards, 2014).

Modeling

Students filed into my classroom, panting from running around in the gym for the last 25 minutes, only to find me standing at the front of the room in a lab coat. No, I wasn't about to do a science experiment; I was about to try a new learning strategy I hadn't tried before, and I was afraid it might be a flop.

"Mr. Wolcott, why are you wearing that long white coat?" Patrick asked.

"Well," I said, "Scientists wear lab coats like this when they are doing experiments, and I am about to try a new teaching strategy with all of you. It might not go so well. So, I want you to realize that scientists make mistakes all the time. It is how they learn. If something goes wrong, and many times it does, they just try again. So, if this lesson doesn't go well, think of it as an experiment, don't be mad at me, and let me try again. Okay?"

Patrick and the others agreed, and I went on with the lesson. As I had hoped, the lesson went fine, but more importantly, I sent a very clear message to my students. We all make mistakes. Mistakes are okay in this room as long as we are trying.

That wouldn't be the last time I used the lab coat in class, and it signaled the start of a culture change in my classroom. Seeing me model that mistakes are part of learning, the students quickly felt more comfortable proclaiming their errors as badges of courage. This was precisely the outcome I was aiming for and the impetus for me laminating little white lab coat cards for each student. When students found themselves in the midst of struggle, they would pull out their "lab coat" and place it on top of the desk. This became an indicator to me and others in the class that the student was trying something out of their comfort zone and wasn't quite sure how it was going. These "lab coat" moments began to facilitate the psychological safety needed for students to grow without fear of retaliation, retribution, or humiliation.

Many might be thinking, "Sounds cute, but older students aren't so easy." I beg to differ. A former graduate student of mine began encouraging her students through modeling in her 11th grade writing class. Each week, she would write a letter to her class explaining her best mistake of the week and what she learned from it. After several weeks, she began to see students become more receptive to feedback and begin seeking help from peers. It was at that time that she changed their weekly Thursday night homework assignment. Rather than have students complete a typical writing task, she asked them to write about their best mistakes. She was shocked when students asked her if they could share in their groups each Friday their writings. Little did she know the weekly assignment would have such an effect. She shared with me how much the class changed, as students were much more participatory, willing to ask for and provide feedback to one another, and prepared to revise and revisit their writing in order to improve it, even when a grade wasn't at stake.

In addition to modeling that mistakes are okay, teachers must model curiosity. Students need to know they can speak up, offer ideas, and ask questions without repercussions. For students with a strong sense of self-efficacy, this isn't a problem. For the vast majority of the remaining students, they will not leave the safety of their comfort zone unless they know there are entering friendly territory.

Two strategies that help enable students to share their ideas safely in the classroom are Wonder Walls and Jot Thoughts. A Wonder Wall is an area within a classroom where students, once prompted with a topic of interest or inquiry, are asked to display their thinking and thoughts around the subject.

Figure 9. Wonder Wall Picture.

Not only do such spaces provide a location for students to share their background knowledge of a topic, but they are also invited to add questions, ideas and share their thinking. Wonder Walls are effective ways for teachers at all grades to promote investigative thinking and support all students in their learning.

Figure 10. Jot Thoughts Picture.

Jot Thoughts, a cooperative learning structure developed by Spencer Kagan, is another excellent way to encourage students to get curious. This strategy calls upon students, once given a topic, to write down as many thoughts as they have about a topic, each on a separate slip of paper or post-it note. When time is up, students then analyze and share their answers. Because thoughts are generated in such a rapid pattern, students aren't worried about having the right answer, just getting their ideas out. Activities such as this provide a safe place for all students to share ideas.

My Best Mistake

One mistake that I made as a teacher was to rely on a behavior chart as a classroom management tool. Students would start the day on green, move to yellow as a warning for their first infraction, miss 10 minutes of recess if they got to orange, and receive a note home to parents if they got to red. Worse yet, I sent a daily report home to parents each night with faces from smiling to frowns indicating the "color" that a student ended up on that day. Although I had great questions posed for parents to ask their child about the day and fun interactive activities on the report, it was the behavior component on the bottom that had the most impact.

Although my "behavior system" worked to curb student behavior in the short term, it didn't mesh with everything else I was trying to accomplish in my classroom. How could I tell students academic mistakes in the classroom were okay, then publicly shame, blame, and defame them when the mistakes happened behaviorally? Call me young, dumb, and hypocritical if you like; I was all of those. This, however, was the best mistake I ever made!

Although I feel guilty to this day that my former students had to endure what I thought was good for them, it taught me a very valuable lesson. Teachers must purposefully align their actions with their desired outcomes. We must critically look at what we say and do, how we set up our classrooms, and determine whether all of these things are working together to produce the psychologically safe conditions that students need to succeed.

Alignment Check

When students come to school each day, their focus isn't on what will be learned that day; their focus is on friendships or lack thereof. With friendship as the primary goal during the school day, learning becomes the secondary one. It isn't until students feel comfortable with those around them that they can devote their mental efforts to what is being taught.

Peer relationships and supports within a classroom are key contributors to school success. Some would argue that peer relationships are the most important relationships in the classroom because students spend the vast majority of their day thinking about or interacting with one another (Hattie & Anderman, 2013).

The brain is social and learns best when interacting with others. Johnson and Johnson (as cited in Hattie & Anderman, 2013) conducted a meta-analysis on peer learning and found that the average student cooperating with another, performed two thirds of a standard deviation above an average student working as an individual. Further, they found that those involved in cooperative partnerships tended to be more involved in activities and tasks, attached greater importance to success, and engaged in more on-task behavior and less apathetic, off-task, and disruptive behaviors (Hattie & Anderman, 2013).

In addition to the increases in academic outcomes associated with strong social support systems, the impact on a child's social-emotional development is equally as evident. Peer relationships provide a unique context in which children learn a range of critical social-emotional skills, such as empathy, cooperation, and problem-solving skills (Pepler & Bierman, 2018).

This should come as no surprise, because learning is enhanced in classrooms where learners have supportive peer-relationships, have a sense of ownership and control over the learning process, and where cultures of camaraderie have been created. It is in these environments that students are provided the ongoing opportunities to work together on challenging activities, collaborate on group projects, assess and confront their own beliefs, discuss the relevance of their learning with one another, and engage in self-discovery.

Why, then, don't more teachers utilize cooperative learning in their classrooms?

The Power of Peers

A quick look inside any classroom yields whether or not the teacher ensures peer support. The litmus test for learning in such an environment comes from whether students are seated in rows or groups. Yes, it is that simple. If we are serious about learning, we must be serious about the seating plan.

Rows originated in the one room schoolhouse and assisted teachers in managing groups of children ranging in age from 5 to 20 years. Individual seating enabled teachers to break up students by subject and level as well as manage the needs of so many.

Then, around the turn of the 20th century, the world developed a mass production mindset. Educators, always being ones to jump on the bandwagon, and wanting to prepare students for the modern workforce, followed suit by keeping rows as well as instituting the production mindset. At the same time, the world was readying for war by mass producing materials and preparing soldiers. Teachers were looking for quick and effective models, and because it worked in the military, many believed it would work in the classroom. Rows are an effective way to transmit information, while also maintaining control of the troops. Despite the advancement of education and the progression of workplace needs, however, this educational model never changed. Rows do not meet the needs of learners. Rather, rows send the message to students that is opposite to what modern education is trying to accomplish; namely, rows signal isolation. They tell students they are on their own, that learning is based on how much they know, their individual abilities, and their current level of intelligence. Rows focus students on immediate skill development and are meant to develop academic growth only.

Courage versus Comfort

The courageous teacher sees that although rows make teaching easier for them, rows do not make learning better for kids. They recognize that group seating such as cooperative learning, sends a message of togetherness, that peers are allies not enemies, that the power of "we" is greater than the power of "me," and that "we" are in this together—"I am here to help you and you are here to help me." Further, co-operative learning lends itself to developing the whole child and lifelong skills like communication and collaboration that are critical for success in the 21st century workplace.

Cooperative Learning Isn't Group Work

Cooperative learning is very different from group work. There is no evidence that seating students in groups alone has any special benefits. Researchers from the Mid-continent Research for Education and Learning (McREL) state, "Cooperative learning structures provide students with opportunities to be a viable part of a collaborative group, where they must work together with roles and deadlines as well as personalities and preferences." These scholars continued, "These skills are vital in today's learning and working environments, especially as those environments become increasingly diverse" (McREL, 2012, p. 45).

High-performing cooperative groups have five things in common. First, such groups rely on face-to-face interaction—students looking at one another as they speak, actively listening, and showing respect, care, and empathy.

Second, all students should be held accountable for learning. They must receive feedback on how their thoughts or work contributed to the learning of others. Next, cooperative learning requires equal participation. Participation is equalized by time or turn. Students get the same number of turns to talk or the same amount of time to talk, either way no one member can dominate.

Cooperative learning also provides time for students to reflect as a team on their effectiveness. What did we learn? How did we learn? Did we work well together? This piece, which is important for group success, is often forgotten in the process.

All of these lead to the final and most important aspect, positive interdependence. Positive interdependence emphasizes that everyone is in the learning together. No one person is more important than another. It is this element that is most important in developing the support systems students need to feel psychologically safe in the classroom. I call this the Three Musketeers Effect: *"All for one and one for all!"*

Ongoing Relationship Development

Although cooperative learning is important for developing the social, emotional and academic skills students needed to be successful in the 21st century, it is not enough to ensure that students develop strong connections with peers. As Martin and Dowson (2009) explained, "A school implementing cooperative learning, mentoring, or an expanded approach to extracurricular activity as its only targeted effort to meet relational needs of its students is unlikely to achieve the interpersonal yields of schools doing more than this" (p. 339).

With this is mind, teachers like those at Scott School make relationship-building a daily activity. They understand the continuing need for students to learn about one another. For some teachers, this occurs by writing whiteboard messages on the board when students walk in, requiring students to share memories or experiences with the class. For others, this involves playing a quick game of "Would You Rather" or answering get-to-know-you questions in a group. Regardless, the orchestrated use of strategies that help students connect has a lasting impact on students' learning and self-worth.

Home Court Advantage

The *home court advantage* is the term used to describe the benefit sports teams have when playing in front of home fans. The impact of psychological effects team members have knowing they will be cheered on and encouraged throughout an athletic contest frees players to perform at their best. When students perceive they have a home court advantage in a particular teacher's classroom, they are more willing to tackle challenging goals, reflect upon and use feedback, and show more agentic engagement. A child who believes that his teachers and peers are on his side is freed—both socially and cognitively—to achieve at high levels.

Whereas many teachers appear to become less caring, less friendly, and less supportive as students get older, the significant ones do the opposite. They create a classroom community that fosters trust with and between students, provides encouragement and support, and leaves students feeling a love for school, a yearning to learn more, and an empowered sense of self.

Reflect/Rethink/Refine

- *In what ways do you provide a psychologically safe environment for your students?*
- *How might you model mistakes are okay for your students?*
- *What is an example of agentic engagement?*
- *What steps can you take to increase the opportunities students have to work with peers in your classroom?*
- *How has your thinking changed about student seating in the classroom?*

ERASE CONFLICT

8 CHAPTER

Maddie's Message:
I know I matter when my teacher works with me to resolve our issues.

In golf, a mulligan is a second chance, a do over, an opportunity to redo a shot. If only we had do-overs in the classroom. I would have loved to have a mulligan to redo a relationship I had with one particular student. Not only for her, but for every other student in my classroom that year.

Toni, an only child, moved to our school 2 months into the year. She had been attending a Montessori school in another state prior to her dad's job transfer. Energetic and full of knowledge, she was eager to show me and everyone else in the class what she knew. She needed constant attention. From the minute she walked in the door in the morning until the moment the bell sounded at the end of the day, she would do anything to quench her craving to have all eyes on her.

As someone who had transferred schools during the academic year several times in my youth, I knew the importance of helping her adjust. We went out of our way to help her feel like she was a member of the family. Unfortunately, nothing we did seemed to help.

As time went on, things didn't get better. Even when I gave her attention, it didn't matter. I tried rewards to get her to stop, and that didn't work. I tried punishments, and that didn't help either. I called parents on the phone and even invited them in to talk, in hopes of learning how I could help her, all to no avail. It got to the point that I would wake up in the middle of the night thinking about her and what I could possibly do to stop the madness, never falling back asleep. I was lost and confused.

The more frustrated I would become with her, the more upset I would become throughout the day. Admittedly, I didn't treat Toni well at times. This worsened the relationship I had with her, as well as with every other student in that room. I didn't understand it at the time, but not only did Toni suffer from my lack of understanding about how to meet her needs, but every child in the room suffered. I learned an incredibly valuable lesson that year; children only feel as safe in the classroom as the worst behaved child is treated. Since I didn't treat Toni well, others didn't feel safe either. My classroom wasn't a good place to be—for me, for the other students, or for Toni.

Climbing Everest

A friend of mine, an avid mountaineer, reminded me that no one who ever attempts to climb Mt. Everest expects perfect weather conditions. Every climber knows to expect a little snow, some rain, and a lot of wind. Therefore, they must be prepared with the right tools so they can react appropriately when each situation arises.

Teaching, like climbing Everest, is no easy feat. There are no perfect students or groups of students, and we educators are not perfect either. Conflict and challenge in the classroom are inevitable. All we can do is be prepared to handle them when they occur without making the situation worse.

Conflict in the Classroom

Research on conflict is quite clear as it relates to relationships. Children who have poor relationships with their teachers demonstrate higher levels of behavior problems, poorer peer relationships, and lower levels of academic achievement (Pianta & Shulman, 2004). Further, students whose relationships with teachers are marked by conflict are less engaged, less likely to enjoy school, and are at greater risk of dropping out of school (Ladd & Burgess, 2001). Relationships based on low levels of conflict are vital to prevent underachievement, especially with boys (Spilt et al., 2011). Teachers consistently report more conflict with boys across all grades. African American boys are particularly at risk (Koepke & Harkins, 2008). Conflict in relationships not only leads to poor academic outcomes, but leaves both teachers and students to feel ineffective and incapable. Spilt et al. (2011) cited Hamre and Pianta's (2005) conclusions that "the findings indicate that relationships with teachers could either narrow or enlarge the achievement gap between at-risk and non-risk students" (p. 14). It is no secret that ending conflict in the classroom is of high priority for student and teacher success.

Start with the ABCs

One night, as my 6-year-old daughter tried to fall asleep, I laid on the floor next to her bed working on my laptop. She looked down as I struggled and asked me why I was having such a difficult time. I explained that I wasn't sure how to start the presentation I was planning. She looked down at me with beautiful blue eyes and said, "Duh, start with the ABCs. Everything starts with the ABCs!" She was right; everything starts with the ABCs.

Self-Determination Theory (SDT) is a theory of motivation developed by Edward Deci and Richard Ryan (1985). The theory, drawn upon heavily throughout this book, is based upon the idea that all people are motivated by three basic psychological needs, the ABCs; autonomy, belonging (often referred as relatedness), and competence.

Deci and Ryan posited that although people are motivated to some extent by external factors, they are more often than not motivated from within as they strive for independence, love and mastery. Further, these authors' research both inside and outside classrooms around the world has proven that when people have their three needs met, they are more creative, more persistent, perform at higher levels, and experience a greater sense of fulfillment in life.

Additionally, Deci and Ryan (1985) showed that the conditions within one's environment either support or thwart the degree to which each need is met. More autonomy-supportive situations foster success, whereas those where needs aren't met negatively affect well-being. Understanding SDT and these basic needs can better prepare teachers when conflict arises within the classroom.

Autonomy. People feel a sense of autonomy when they have control over what they are doing and have the ability to move forward as they see best. Perceived control of behavior or freedom to act creates deeper ownership and increased motivation. Acting on one's own regard rather than being told to do something enables one to perceive choice in what they are doing.

The opposite of autonomy is coercion. It should not be a surprise that no one likes to be forced to do things against their will. Students who never experience autonomy often act out when told to do something, feeling they are being pressured to do something against their will. Although no teacher wants to coerce a child into compliance, there are times in the classroom when students do need to act as we need them to. In these situations, author Daniel Pink (2011) suggested that educators turn "every chore into a choice." Pink also recommended that teachers provide choices via one of the "Four Ts": Task (what they are doing), Time (when they will do something or when it will be due), Technique (how they may do something, i.e., on paper or computer), or Team (with whom they will do something, alone or with a partner).

Over the past decade, teachers around the country have begun to see the benefits of providing students more "voice and choice" over their assignments. Sadly, with best intentions at heart, many students do not benefit from the autonomy because they are provided with "too much" autonomy. Without proper guidance and support, too much autonomy can be detrimental, as I will discuss in the section concerning competence.

Belonging. Often referred to as relatedness, belonging describes one's need to feel cared for and connected to others. Everyone wants to love and be loved by those around them. Feeling that we matter in the lives of those we work with and learn with makes us feel that we are part of something bigger than just ourselves. Having positive relationships with both teachers and peers creates a greater sense of belonging within students.

Dweck et al. (2014) attributed much to such relationships stating, a sense of belonging allows students to rise above the concerns of the moment and is linked to long-term student motivation and school success" (p. 11).

One of the most important ways in which students can experience a sense of belonging is by having a best friend. Best friends are a source of interpersonal support, as well as a source of beliefs and values. Having a trusting, caring, and close relationship with a best friend improves social and emotional adjustment (Nelson & DeBacker, 2008). Hattie (2014) further noted that in studies looking at students who move schools, "The single greatest predictor of subsequent school success is whether the student makes a friend in the first month" (p. 188). Students who are not accepted by peers in their class are reliant on teachers to intervene and model acceptance. No child should feel rejected and alone.

A simple strategy that many schools I work with use to ensure students have a best friend requires only 30 minutes of time and a class list. At the end of the first full month of school, teachers are asked to print off a list of all students in their class. Then, next to each students' name, they are asked to list one or two friends that they know the student has in class. If the teacher is unable to list a friend for each child, the teacher's goal becomes to find a friend for that child. Although this is more easily done at the elementary school level where teachers spend the entire day with each child, I have seen this strategy executed just as effectively at both the middle and high school level.

Competence. Have you ever experienced a child spontaneously doing an arm pump and saying "yes" when they have done well on an assignment or test? This is competence; this is the feeling of mastery. We all want to feel effective, successful, and optimally challenged. When we feel that we have the ability to perform, make progress, and excel at a task, we experience a heightened state of self-worth. Those feelings trigger us to want to do more and take on the next challenge.

Niemiec and Ryan (2009) suggested that teachers spend considerable focus on providing activities that optimally challenge students. Working on tasks that are at this level allows students to test and expand their capabilities, while building knowledge and confidence along the way. Additionally, these researchers highlighted the importance of providing individualized feedback to students during the learning episode to build student feelings of self-efficacy. When students are on winning streaks, they are more likely to tackle more difficult and challenging activities.

Students are aided in feeling competent when working in structured environments. In classrooms where structure is lacking, failure fills this void. This leaves students unsure of what to do and how to proceed in learning. Their want to be successful is thwarted when working or learning in chaos. As detrimental as this is for students in the classroom, educators who reflect upon the home lives of students can begin to paint a better picture of why some students have such difficulty at school.

Children who regularly go home to chaos have a tendency to struggle with the slightest bit of structure when they enter a classroom. It isn't because they don't want to work within the boundaries provided; it is more likely that they don't know how to or haven't had enough opportunities. It is imperative that educators provide students support, encouragement and patient guidance while they ease students into the structured routines of the classroom.

Stimulus> Choice> Response

"Between stimulus and response, there is a space. In that space is our power to choose our response. In our response lies our growth and our freedom" (Viktor Frankl).

In the years since working with Toni, I have learned a lot about how conflicts in the classroom start and how they can be prevented. That knowledge begins with the quote above by Holocaust survivor and famed Austrian psychiatrist, Viktor Frankl.

All classroom conflict begins with some stimulus. Frequently undetected by the teacher, the stimulus triggers an emotional need (one of the ABCs) within the child. The child is unable to properly process the information and consciously choose an appropriate response, and reacts instantaneously. Outward responses are frequently described as externalizing behaviors. Such behaviors include acting out, non-compliance, talking out, physical aggression, or other conduct-based disruptions. These are usually very apparent to all when they occur. Inward responses are more difficult for teachers to recognize and thus address. Often referred to as internalizing behaviors, anxiety, withdrawal, sadness, and depression may go unnoticed in the classroom.

Externalizing behaviors are the most common cause of teacher-student conflict in the classroom. Such encounters also lead to heightened turmoil as they often negatively impact the classroom climate and impeded the learning of all students. Fortunately, conflict created by outward displays of student emotion follow a predictable pattern. When recognized, it can be stopped; if not halted, this vicious cycle can interrupt and setback learning for hours, days, or even months.

As Frankl noted, the cycle begins with a stimulus. The stimulus triggers an emotion within the student. That emotion is based upon one of the child's basic needs not being met. Because the need isn't met, the child responds, sometimes consciously, other times unconsciously. The child's behavioral response to the incident then serves as a stimulus, eliciting a reflex within the teacher. An emotion is triggered within the teacher. A response then occurs based upon whether the teacher's personal needs are being met. A teacher in control of her emotions can then choose her response. One who feels threatened, however, may unfortunately react without conscious thought. The cycle either ends there or—unfortunately, all too often in situations like mine from the start of the chapter—continues. Let's take a look at an example of this in action.

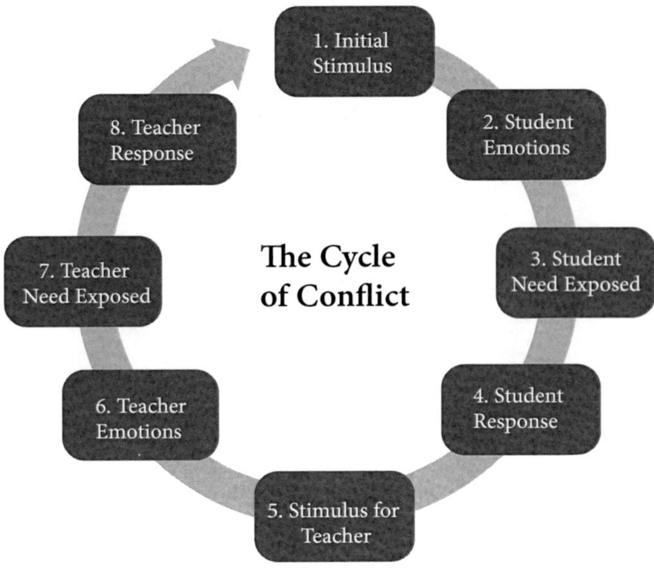

Figure 11. The cycle of conflict.

- Initial Stimulus
  - Toni is not called upon when she raises her hand.

- Student Emotion
  - "I wasn't called on because he doesn't think I know the answer."

- Student Need Exposed
  - "I am not competent."

- Student Response
  - Toni blurts out the answer.

- Resulting Stimulus for the Teacher
  - Classroom discussion is interrupted by Toni's blurting out.

- Teacher Emotion
  - "She keeps yelling out because she wants to get her way."

- Teacher Need Exposed
  - "She is so coercive. This impacts my sense of autonomy"

- Teacher Response
  - "Toni, you must stop blurting out. It isn't your turn."

In some situations, the child will obey the teacher directive and the cycle of conflict will be paused momentarily. Many times, however, the dance of discord continues. The response of the teacher elicits additional feelings within the student and the cycle continues. Without a resolution, the occurrence becomes a daily struggle as neither person recognizes the impact the situation has on the other person. A continual back and forth ensues.

Caught Up in the Rhythm of It

When emotion meets emotion, no one wins. It becomes very simple for teachers to get caught up in the rhythm of the cycle, with one response feeding the next. As the more powerful figure in the classroom, it is all too easy for many teachers to blame, shame, and defame the troublesome student in front of other students. Such incidences distort, disregard, and dissolve relationships, not only between the teacher and student, but between the teacher and other students as well. Especially in older grades, most students have a tendency to side with the student in such circumstances. Not wanting to address issues at hand, some teachers choose to retreat, which is equally disruptive to learning.

When They Go Low, We Go High

To understand the responses above, educators must be reminded of a few basic brain facts. The brain is made up of three regions: the brainstem, the limbic system, and the prefrontal cortex. The first two regions make up the lower part of the brain, and work together to help regulate emotions and a person's fight, flight, freeze or faint response. Fight (attacking) and flight (defending) are typical externalizing responses. Freezing (surrendering) and fainting (hiding/avoiding) are characterized as internalizing responses. The latter region, the frontal region, is the higher part of the brain, which is responsible for executive functioning, including seeing things from another's perspective, choosing how to respond to situations, and solving problems. When students experience an amygdala hijack, getting caught up in emotional responses originating in the lower part of the brain, educators must "go high" and consciously focus on responding with the upper regions of our brains. We do this by viewing student behavior as communication, and asking ourselves, "What is the student's behavior telling us about their needs?" By consciously choosing our response to student behavior, rather than impulsively reacting to the situation, teachers are better able to stop conflict in its tracks and help students succeed academically, as well as socially and emotionally.

The STORY Map

One tool educators that can use to stop the Cycle of Conflict is the STORY Map. This resource assists teachers in determining which of the ABCs is the root cause of a student's actions. Although many teachers prefer to complete the map on their own, a more effective way is to fill it out with colleagues who do not know the child or have as close of relationship. Colleagues can prompt the referring teacher to reflect upon the student by going through each letter of the map. This allows teachers to more critically assess student needs and behaviors. Whether teachers choose to use the STORY Map or another tool to end the conflict, it's important for teachers to spend time building up the relationship with the student at the same time.

Hamre and Pianta (2001; 2005) have consistently shown that closer teacher-student relationships result in lower levels of classroom conflict. This is particularly important for teachers working with older students, as middle and high school students typically hold on to negative interactions and conflicts with their teachers longer than younger students.

Internalizing Behaviors

Although students who exhibit internalizing behaviors may not necessarily experience outward conflict with the teacher, there is often a lack of closeness in the relationship. Many would say that these behaviors that aren't as easily recognized are more detrimental to student health and well-being than the easily noticed externalizing behaviors.

It is not uncommon, due to the hectic pace of the school day, for such behaviors to be overlooked. Sadly, the percentage of students suffering from depression, stress, and anxiety is on the rise. According to Ramin Mojtabai, professor at Johns Hopkins School of Public Health, the odds of adolescents suffering from clinical depression grew by 37% between 2005 and 2014 (Sugarman, 2017). This research serves as further evidence that teachers should make relationship-building a priority. Teachers who know their students well are more likely to notice slight mood changes or irregularities in student conduct. Additionally, in times of crisis, students are more likely to turn to a trusted teacher than a parent to talk.

The 3RT

It is evident that teachers should strive to have solid relationships with each student with whom they teach. Too often educators don't take the time to sit down and reflect upon the strength of the relationship they have with each student. One way for teachers to assess the quality of relationship they have with each child is the Relationship Rating Reflection Tool (3RT). Teachers can designate the strength of the connection they have with each child by shading in bars on the battery scale; zero bars indicate a weak to negative relationship, and five bars shows an incredibly positive relationship. After completing the scale for each child, teachers are encouraged to determine a goal for maintaining or strengthening the relationship with each student. Like all relationships, teacher-student bonds have ebbs and flows during the school year. For this reason, the 3RT is best utilized twice per year.

Another way that educators have used the 3RT is to ask students to rate their perceptions of the teacher-student relationship. Koepke and Harkins (2008) noted that both boys and girls viewed relationships with their teachers as being significantly less close than the teachers reported. They explained that data indicates gender disparities in child ratings of conflict and overall relational health, such that boys rated their relationships with teachers as being significantly more conflicted and less healthy than girls' ratings (Koepke & Harkins, 2008). A copy of the 3RT Student Form is available at www.significant72.com.

Learn Why

Although conflicts will inevitably occur in the classroom throughout the year, teachers who are able to "learn from" instead of "react to" what happens in the classroom stand the best chance of improving educational outcomes. If teachers can use students' patterns of action in the classroom to diagnose underlying motivational issues, they can respond to disaffected students in ways that are more likely to renew their intrinsic motivation and improve their relationships with teachers and peers (Furrer, Skinner, & Pitzer, 2014). The fastest route through conflict comes through strong connections between the teacher and the child.

Reflect/Rethink/Refine

- *What student would you like to use a mulligan to "do over" your relationship?*
- *Which of your ABCs is most affected by conflict with students?*
- *How would you explain the cycle of conflict to a colleague who hasn't read this book yet?*
- *What would you learn about your relationships with students after completing the 3RT?*
- *How might you and your colleagues use the STORY Map to better determine the needs of challenging students?*

Relationship Rating Reflection Tool

Teacher:____________________ Grade/Course: __________________

Directions: Please reflection upon each teacher-student relationship in the classroom. For each child, rate the strength of the connection using the battery scale below. The more positive the connection, the more bars should be shaded in on the scale. Develop an individualized goal for each student as necessary.

Student: ________________
Goal: __________________

Student: ________________
Goal: __________________

Student: ________________
Goal: __________________

Student: ________________
Goal: __________________

Student: ________________
Goal: __________________

Student: ________________
Goal: __________________

Student: ________________
Goal: __________________

Student: ________________
Goal: __________________

Student: ________________
Goal: __________________

Free templates available for download at www.significant72.com.

Toni's STORY Map

The *STORY Map* can be used whenever a teacher feels the need to take a closer look at a student's social, emotional or academic needs. Teachers complete each box of the map in order from one to five, carefully reflecting throughout.

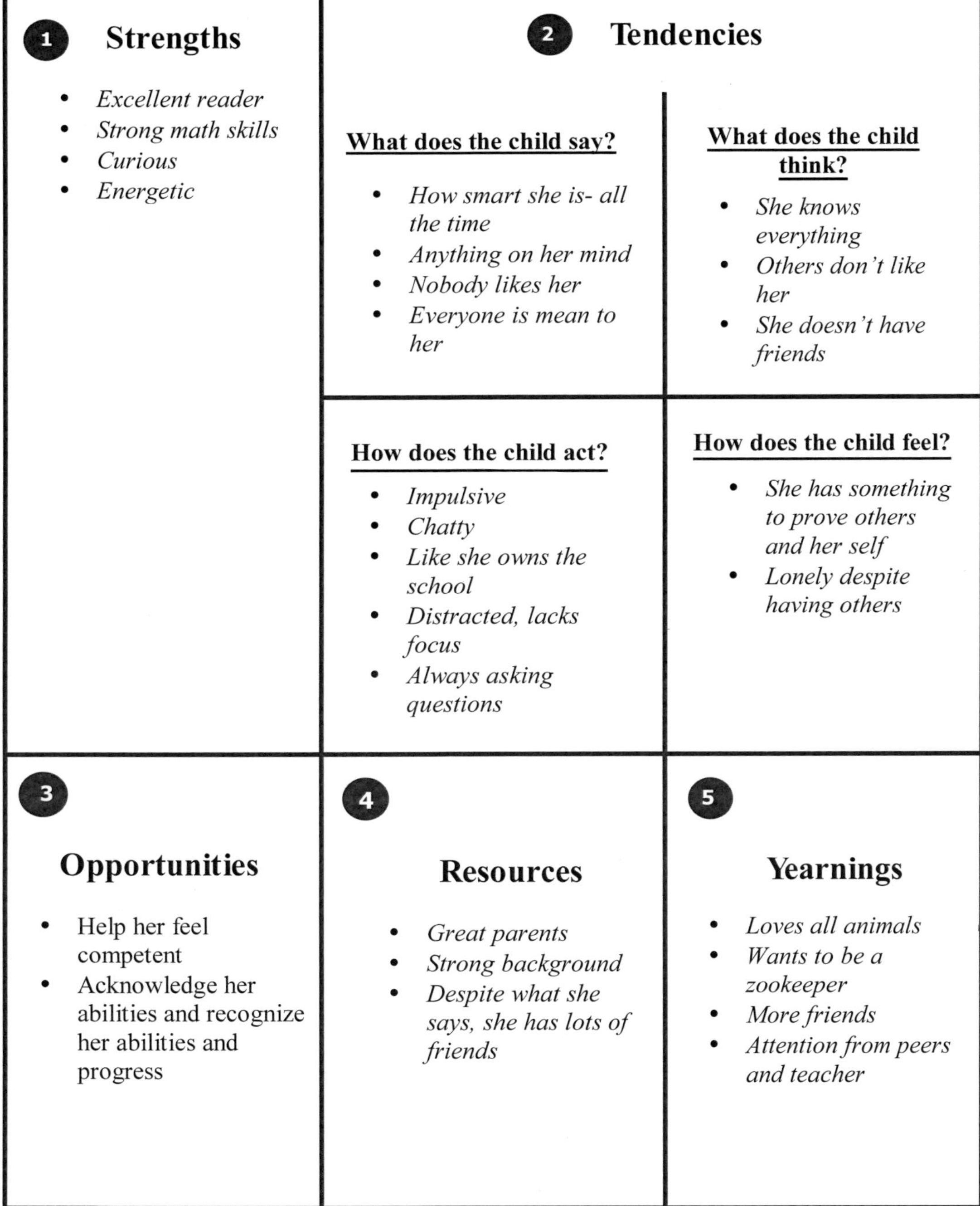

1 Strengths

- *Excellent reader*
- *Strong math skills*
- *Curious*
- *Energetic*

2 Tendencies

What does the child say?

- *How smart she is- all the time*
- *Anything on her mind*
- *Nobody likes her*
- *Everyone is mean to her*

What does the child think?

- *She knows everything*
- *Others don't like her*
- *She doesn't have friends*

How does the child act?

- *Impulsive*
- *Chatty*
- *Like she owns the school*
- *Distracted, lacks focus*
- *Always asking questions*

How does the child feel?

- *She has something to prove others and her self*
- *Lonely despite having others*

3 Opportunities

- Help her feel competent
- Acknowledge her abilities and recognize her abilities and progress

4 Resources

- *Great parents*
- *Strong background*
- *Despite what she says, she has lots of friends*

5 Yearnings

- *Loves all animals*
- *Wants to be a zookeeper*
- *More friends*
- *Attention from peers and teacher*

Free templates available for download at www.significant72.com.

THE COURAGE TO ACT

CHAPTER 9

Maddie's Message:
I know I matter when all of my teachers make relationship-building a priority.

As I drove out of town, I knew the day that I had just spent with staff at Henderson High School was special. Yes, most schools I work with are excited about strengthening the relationships between students and staff, but it seemed different there. The intensity to which they collaborated during breakout activities and the depth of the questions they asked showed that this group meant business. They were on a mission to relate to each and every child within the school. Two months later, I found out how serious they were.

As I sat at the airport in Rapid City, South Dakota, awaiting a flight home, my phone rang. The principal of Henderson was on the phone. He wanted to give me an update on his school's progress over the first 8 weeks. After several minutes of small talk, he said, "Greg, something happened here that you need to know about." The tone in his voice changed.

He told me about a relationship-building activity that they had undertaken. In order to ensure that each student had a significant adult connection, he and his leadership team had posted pictures of all 2,000 students on the walls of their faculty lounge. Then, during a faculty meeting, they charged staff with putting what they had learned about relationships into place.

A member of the leadership team introduced the staff to relationship mapping. Armed with three colors of sticky dots from the local office supply stores, staff were directed over the course of the next 6 weeks to place a yellow dot on the corner of each child's picture with whom they felt they had a strong connection. They were then asked to place a green dot over the yellow dot when they felt they knew the student so well they could strike up a conversation in the hallway. And finally, they were told to put a blue dot on the pictures of students they had such a strong bond with that they could carry on a non-school related discussion with the child at the local grocery store. Their goal was for each student to have at least a yellow sticker by Halloween and a green one by winter break.

Throughout the first quarter of the year, it was evident that staff were taking the initiative seriously. Almost every picture had a yellow dot, and there were hundreds of green- and blue-dotted pictures.

The school improvement team—composed of department heads, school administrators, and counselors—met in the lounge the Friday before Halloween to review the school's progress. After briefly celebrating how many students had yellow and green dots next to their pictures, the group realized that there were still approximately 60 students who did not have any stickers. Recognizing that they still had work to do, the team divided the remaining pictures up amongst each other and set about trying to make initial connections with the final students.

One member of the group, the school's head basketball coach and physical education department chair, immediately went about meeting with each of the students on his list. He scoured the halls until he found each one. Then, he held a brief conversation with each. One particular encounter that the coach had was the purpose of the principal's phone call to me.

The coach found one of the boys on his list standing alone outside the school's auditorium and invited him to chat. The boy, caught off guard, reluctantly agreed. The coach then initiated the conversation by telling the boy how he'd seen him in the hallway and had wanted to say "hi" for several weeks, but had been so busy with the start of the year that he hadn't had the opportunity. The boy was taken aback and surprised that the coach had even noticed him. The coach reinforced the fact that he had noticed the boy on numerous occasions, perceived that the boy seemed like a great kid, and decided that he was someone that he wanted to get to know. The two hit it off immediately.

About 10 minutes into the conversation, the boy began to tear up. The coach asked the boy if he was okay. The tears came down the 16-year-old's face at a faster rate, as he told the coach that he didn't think anybody at the school noticed him or even cared about him. The coach reassured the boy that the school was full of adults who cared, and that he was just one of many.

After wiping the tears off of his face, the boy reached into his pocket and pulled out a bag of pills. He explained to the coach that it was his intention to commit suicide after school that day. In tears, the boy collapsed into the coach's arms.

Several minutes later, an ambulance arrived, and the two rode to the hospital together. I had tears of my own as the principal relayed the story to me. I was so proud of the efforts of the staff at the school, and most importantly of that coach.

At the end of the school year, I received another call from the principal. He informed me of how impactful that event was on the staff at the school, and how much the culture had changed. No child would ever lack a positive adult connection in that school. Additionally, he let me know that after several weeks of out-of-school therapy and treatment, the boy was back at school.

He became a manager on the school basketball team so he could stay connected with the coach. As a freshman and sophomore, the boy had been earning "D" letter grades, but was now maintaining a solid "B" average in all of his classes. More importantly, he now had the adult connection that he so desperately needed.

As educators, we never know where our influence ends. We get so caught up in what we are doing that we don't often stop and realize why we're doing what we're doing. It is up to us to develop the relationship that students need to conquer the world they face.

Everyone Needs a Cornerman

I love all of the Rocky movies. Although I am a huge fan of underdogs, Rocky isn't my favorite character. My favorite character is Mickey. Mickey, the old grizzled trainer, epitomizes the courageous teacher described within the pages of this book. Throughout training, Mickey was there at Rocky's side, pushing him and encouraging through the struggle, yet providing encouragement at the same time. When Rocky would get knocked down or when he felt like he was ready to quit, it was Mickey's voice in his head that prompted him to get back up and give it more effort. Every student deserves a cornerman, someone like Mickey. They deserve to have an adult in their corner that believes in them more than they might even believe in themselves.

The benefits of such an adult are many for all children, but particularly for students at risk of school failure. Harvard's Center on the Developing Child (2015) stated, "Whether the burdens come from the hardships of poverty, the challenges of parental substance abuse or serious mental illness, the stresses of war, the threats of recurrent violence or chronic neglect, or a combination of factors, the single most common finding is that children who end up doing well have had at least one stable and committed relationship with a supportive parent, caregiver, or other adult" (p. 1). They continued, "These relationships provide the personalized responsiveness, scaffolding, and protection that buffer children from developmental disruption" (p. 1).

With this in mind, all schools should take a more proactive approach to ensuring that every student has an adult connection. Whether replicating the relationships mapping activity above or coming up with a different method of connecting teachers and students, it is imperative that all students have an adult that they can turn to, gather strength from, and who will always have their back. Some students find that person at home, others find the person at school, in an after-school program, during music or band activities, or elsewhere. When students have such a relationship, their chances of success are heightened.

Protective and Predictive

In their seminal study, McGrath and Van Bergen (2014) concluded that teacher-student relationships are both protective and predictive. They summarized their findings with the following:

For students at-risk of negative teacher-student relationships, experiencing a positive relationship with a teacher can protect against numerous other negative influences including maladaptive behavior, negative life events, poor quality child-parent relationships, and referral to special education. It can also predict a range of behavioral and academic outcomes; not just within the school years, but perhaps also in adulthood. For example, those with negative teacher-student relationships may be more likely to be unemployed in adulthood, whereas those with positive relationships may experience a higher degree of success. The predictive and protective functions of the teacher-student relationship suggest that one positive relationship may be sufficient to alter the trajectory of a student at risk of negative outcomes (pp. 13-14).

Knowing the protective and predictive natural of relationships between the student and the teacher, I have created the "Teacher-Student Relationship At-Risk Checklist" for school staff to use to determine if students within their classroom or school are more likely to have negative relationships with their teachers, thus resulting in negative school outcomes.

The checklist is simple to use. Teachers answer each question and allocated points based upon the answer to each. The more points a student receives on the at-risk checklist above, the more likely the student is to have a negative teacher-student relationship. School staff should place particular focus on cultivating strong relationships with students who score high. The "2x4" strategy described in Chapter 2 is particularly helpful for forming bonds with all students, including those at risk.

Frequently teachers may utilize the checklist with all students within a classroom. In such cases, classrooms with higher overall point totals should consider allocating additional time to class building and team building activities to help strengthen connections with and between students. Sample activities can be found at www.significant72.com.

Teacher-Student Relationship At-Risk Checklist		
Student:	**Date of Birth:**	
Teacher:	**Grade:**	
Is the student:		
• Male		If yes, add 1 point
• African American or Hispanic		If yes, add 1 point
• Absent more than 10% of the school year		If yes, add 1 point
• In middle or high school		If yes, add 1 point
• In a transition year *(kindergarten, first year of middle school or first year of high school)*		If yes, add 1 point
Does the student:		
• Receive special education services		If yes, add 1 point
• Receive free or reduced lunch		If yes, add 1 point
• Perform in the lowest quarter of the class		If yes, add 1 point
• Behave poorly		If yes, add 1 point
• Have a low parent involvement		If yes, add 1 point
	Total Points	
1-3 points Slight Risk, 4-6 Moderate Risk, 7-10 points High Risk		

The Yin and the Yang

You have probably seen the symbol consisting of a small black and white circle before—maybe on a notebook, a bumper sticker, or on someone's shoulder in the form of a tattoo. This image, which dates back thousands of years, serves as the perfect metaphor for the thoughts, ideas, and attitudes discussed throughout this book.

In Chinese culture, the yin and yang symbol represents how seemingly opposite or contrary ideas may actually be complementary, interconnected, and interdependent. Yin is the "shady side;" it is dark, negative, and feminine. Yang is the "sunny side," which is considered bright, positive, and more masculine. The two halves swirl into one another to form a balanced, harmonious wholeness. Inside each is a dot of the opposite color. This symbolizes the fact that within the negative, there is positive, and within the positive, there is negative.

Each quality contains the beginning point for the other. Like sky and earth, water and fire, day and night, both are needed for balance. Without both, equilibrium cannot exist.

The same can be said for the two key concepts needed to be a "Significant Sally." The courageous teacher comprises high levels of care and press, two seemingly opposing ideas. Further, in care, the more feminine aspect of teaching, there is also press. "If I didn't care, I wouldn't press you so hard for excellence." In press, often considered the more masculine/firm aspect of teaching, there is still care. "If I didn't press you hard to excel, I wouldn't be showing you that I care." It is the dynamic interaction of the two that brings harmony to the classroom; as balance is restored, so is student success.

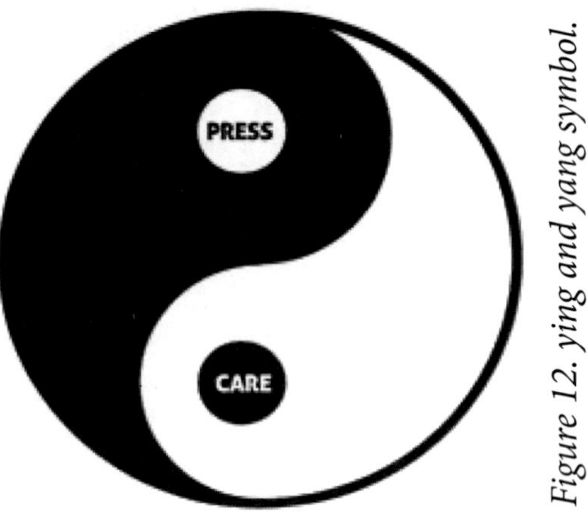

Figure 12. ying and yang symbol.

The yin and yang concept is visible throughout the book, as the dynamic interplay of both care and press can be found in each chapter:

- We work to connect with students because we want to get to know them, and by getting to know them we can push them.
- We obsess over the press because we want to challenge students to do their best, because we care about their long-term success.
- We unleash clarity so children better understand what is to be learned, and because we don't want unproductive struggle to negatively impact their learning.
- We raise the relevance of what students are learning in order to increase their motivation, as by doing so allows us to use more challenging content.
- We accelerate achievement not only so students feel good about themselves, but so we can push them to tackle more difficult tasks.
- We guarantee support on the grounds that a more psychologically safe environment will make them feel more comfortable, yet at the same time provide the conditions for us to push them to excel.
- We erase conflict because we want students to know they are respected, but also because we know that without a solid relationship, we cannot help students achieve at the academic levels they need to be successful.

The meaning of yin and yang goes slightly deeper in ancient Chinese philosophy. The symbol also represents the starting point for change. It is my greatest hope that this book will serve as a starting point for educators to change their practices and place courage before comfort in all they do, forming strong relationships with every student they teach.

Your Mission, if You Choose to Accept It

One of the highlights of my day is when I get into classrooms and see my incredibly talented colleagues in action. I vividly recall one particular visit to a third-grade classroom. Having just read Bernard Weber's *Courage*, students were writing and sharing times in their lives when they had demonstrated courage. Their writings were amazing, as were their 9-year-old definitions of courage:

- *"Courage is to be brave and to face your fear of going on a rollercoaster."*
- *"Courage is going to the deepest part of the pool at the waterpark, without a life jacket on."*
- *"Courage is going downstairs when the lights are off."*
- *"Courage is when I first learned gymnastics. I wasn't good at it. And the next thing I knew after I practiced lots, I won a trophy and I was excited!"*

My question to you is, how do you define courage?

It takes courage to develop a relationship mindset in today's educational landscape. Teachers must realize that it takes time and ongoing effort. These are two things that are tough to expend and which we don't have much of, given the current demands. Courage doesn't happen by accident, but through purposeful planning, intentional design, and daily execution.

Courage comes from waking up every morning, looking ourselves in the mirror, and asking one simple question:

What can I do today to make sure the time students spend in my classroom is the best part of their day?

I assure you that if you do this, not only will your students thrive in the classroom, but you will as well!

Good luck, and…

#UnleashAwesomeness!

Significant 72: Month-by-Month Implementation

Implementing Significant 72 is an easy process. All that is required is a team of dedicated staff who want to develop significant relationships with and between their students. This team must intentionally integrate opportunities throughout the year. A month-by-month model with ideas is provided below.

Significant 72 Success Checklist		
Month	**Activity**	**Description**
August	First Three Days	The first 3 days are the most important days of the school year. Teachers should utilize a variety of whole class and small group relationship-building activities in order to get to know their students and for students to get to know one another. Ideas can be found at www.significant72.com.
September	Best Friend Survey	Among the greatest predictors of a child's success is whether or not they have a friend within the first month of school. Teachers should print a copy of their class roster and try and identify each student's best friend in the classroom. Teachers should attempt to find friends for students who do not have one.
October	Relationship Reflection Rating Tool (3RT)	Teachers should complete the 3RT for each student in their class. Once complete, teachers should attempt to further develop relationships with students rated less strongly.
November	Panorama Classroom Teacher-Student Relationship Survey	Teachers in grades 3-12 can administer the brief five question survey to gauge how students are feeling about their relationships with the classroom teacher. The survey can be downloaded at www.panoramaed.com or www.significant72.com.
	Whole School Relationship Mapping	Ensuring every child has a cornerman is crucial in a Significant 72 school. The Relationship Mapping Strategy developed by researchers at Harvard University, used in the Wall of Students example can be found at www.significant72.com.
December	First Day Back Activities	December is a challenging month for many students, particularly those who live in at-risk households. Intentional relationship-building after Thanksgiving helps during this difficult month.
January	First Day Back	The first day back after Winter Break serves as a chance for students to reconnect and for staff to lay out expectations for the second half of the year.
	First Day- New Semester	Similar to the start of the year, the first day of a new semester should be used for initial connection. Any time students have a new teacher and new classmates is an opportunity to promote connection.
February	Panorama Classroom Belonging Survey	Teachers in grades 3-12 can administer the brief five question survey to gauge how valued students feel by their classmates. This survey is a great predictor of psychological safety. The survey can be downloaded at www.panoramaed.com or www.significant72.com.

March	Relationship Reflection Rating Tool (3RT)	In February, teachers are encouraged to once again rate their relationships with each student and purposefully plan ways to enhance relationship based on results
April	First Day Back	The first day back after Spring Break is an opportunity for staff to reconnect students as well as remind students
May	Personal Notes	Teachers can take time to write a personal note to each student in the class, highlighting memories from the year.
Ongoing	Whole Class Relationship-building	All teachers should strive to conduct one to two 10 to 15-minute whole class relationship-building activities each week throughout the school year.
Ongoing	Small Group Relationship-building	All teachers should attempt to conduct daily 3- to 5-minute small group relationship-building activities each week throughout the school year.
Ongoing	Passion Period	Teachers are encouraged to spend 15-30 minutes a month sharing a personal passion with students. Personal Disclosure in this way allows students more deeply connect with their teachers.
Ongoing	"2 x 4"	Teachers spend 2 minutes a day with four different students. The purpose of each session is to connect with each child as student first. Teachers should refrain from talking about school. Sample conversation topics can be found at www.significant72.com.
Ongoing	Leader Modeling	Building leadership should model relationship-building strategies during faculty meetings and professional development. These activities will not only develop stronger bonds between colleagues, but will add tools and strategies to teacher relationship tool boxes.
As Needed	STORY Map	Teachers wanting to problem solve the needs of individual students should use this tool as needed to put an end to the Cycle of Conflict.

REFERENCES

Achor, S. (2018). *Big potential.* New York, NY: Random House.

Allensworth, E. M., Farrington, C. A., Gordon, M. F., Johnson, D. W., Klein, K., McDaniel, B., & Nagaoka, J. (2018). *Supporting social, emotional, & academic development: Research implications for educators.* Chicago, IL: University of Chicago Consortium on School Research.

Amabile, T., & Kramer, S. (2011). *The progress principle.* Boston, MA: Harvard Business Review Press.

Ausubel, D. P. (1968). *Educational psychology: A cognitive view.* New York, NY: Holt, Rinehart and Winston.

Bandura, A. (1977). *Self-efficacy: The exercise of control.* New York, NY: Freeman.

Baumeister, R. F., & Leary, M. R. (1995). The need to belong: Desire for interpersonal attachments as a fundamental human motivation. *Psychological Bulletin,* 117, 497-529.

Baumrind, D. (1968). Authoritarian vs. authoritative parental control. *Adolescence, 3,* 255-272.

Braiker, H. (2001). *The disease to please.* Boston, MA: McGraw-Hill.

Brophy, J. (2005). Goal theorists should move on from performance goals. *Educational Psychologist, 40,* 167-176.

Buyse, E., Verschueren, K., Verachtert, P., & Van Damme, J. (2009). Predicting school adjustment in early elementary school: Impact of teacher-child relationship quality and relational classroom climate. *Elementary School Journal, 110,* 1.

Center on the Developing Child at Harvard University. (2015). *Supportive Relationships and Active Skill-Building Strengthen the Foundations of Resilience:* Working Paper No. 13. Retrieved from http://www.developingchild.harvard.edu

Chang, M. L. (2009). An appraisal perspective of teacher burnout: Examine the emotional work of teachers. *Education Psychology Review, 21,* 193-218.

Cohen, G. L., & Garcia, J. (2014). Educational theory, practice and policy and the wisdom of social psychology. *Policy Insights from the Behavioral and Brain Sciences, 1(1)*, 13-20.

Cook, C. R., Fiat, A., Larson, M., Daikos, C., Slemrod, T., Holland, E. A., ... Renshaw, T. (2018). Positive greetings at the door: Evaluation of a low-cost, high-yield proactive classroom management strategy. *Journal of Positive Behavior Interventions, 20(3)*, 149-159.

Cooper, H. M. (1983). *A historical overview of teacher expectation effects.* Paper presented at the Annual Convention of the American Psychological Association, California.

Cooper, K. S., & Miness, A. (2014). The co-creation of caring student-teacher relationships: Does teacher understanding matter? *High School Journal, 97(4)*, 264-290.

Cornelius-White, J. (2007). Learner-centered teacher-student relationships are effective: A meta-analysis. *Review of Educational Research, 77(1)*, 113-143.

Cruickshank, D. R., Kennedy, J. J., Bush, A., & Myers, B. (1979). Clear teaching: What is it? *British Journal of Teacher Education, 5(1)*, 27-33.

Davis, H. A. (2001). The quality and impact of relationships between elementary school students and teachers. *Contemporary Educational Psychology, 26*, 431-453.

Davis, H. A. (2003). Conceptualizing the role and influence of student-teacher relationships on children's social and cognitive development. *Educational Psychologist, 38*, 207-234.

Davis, H. A. (2006). Exploring the contexts of relationship quality between middle school students and teachers. *Elementary School Journal, 106*, 193-223.

Davis, H. A., & Bischoff, A. B. (2009, April). *Exploring the nature of teacher warmth and demand for high achieving, low-income urban students on science motivation.* Paper presented at the annual conference of the American Educational Research Association, San Diego, CA.

Dean, C. B., Hubbell, E. R., Pitler, H., & Stone, B. (2012). *Classroom instruction that works: Research-based strategies for increasing student achievement* (2nd ed.). Alexandria, VA: Association for Supervision and Curriculum Development.

Deci, E. L., & Ryan, R. M. (1985). *Intrinsic motivation and self-determination in human behavior.* New York, NY: Plenum.

Deci, E. L., Vallerand, R. J., Pelletier, L. G., & Ryan, R. M. (1991). Motivation and education: The self-determination perspective. *Educational Psychologist, 26*, 325-346.

Delich, N. A., & Roberts, S. D. (2017). Empowering students through the application of self-efficacy theory in school social work: An intervention model. *International Journal of School Social Work, 2(1)*, 1.

Delpit, L. (1995). *Other people's children: Cultural conflict in the classroom.* New York, NY: New Press.

Dweck, C. S. (2000). *Self-theories: Their role in motivation, personality and develoment.* New York, NY: Psychology Press.

Dweck, C. (2006). *Mindset: The new psychology of success.* New York, NY: Random House.

Dweck, C., Walton, G., & Cohen, G. (2014). *Academic tenacity: Mindsets and skills that promote long-term learning.* Seattle, WA: Bill & Melinda Gates Foundation.

Eccles, J. (1983). Expectancies, values, and academic behaviors. In J. Spence (Ed.), *Achievement and achievement motives (pp. 75-146)*. San Francisco, CA: Freemen.

Eccles, J. S., & Barber, B. L. (1999). Student council, volunteering, basketball, or marching band: What kind of extracurricular involvement matters? *Journal of Adolescent Research, 14(1)*, 10-43.

Edwards, J. (2014). The role of the music therapist in promoting parent infant attachment. *Canadian Journal of Music Therapy, 20(1)*, 38-38.

Edwards, S., & Edick, N. (2013). Culturally responsive teaching for significant relationships. *Journal of Praxis in Multicultural Education, 7(1).*

Elias, M. J., & Haynes, N. M. (2008). Social competence, social support, and academic achievement in minority, low-income, urban elementary school children. *School Psychology Quarterly, 23*, 474-495.

Farrington, C. A. (2013). *Academic mindsets as a critical component of deeper learning.* Chicago, IL: University of Chicago.

Farrington, C. A., Roderick, M., Allensworth, E., Nagaoka, J., Keyes, T. S., Johnson, D. W., & Beechum, N. O. (2012). *Teaching adolescents to become learners: The role of noncognitive factors in shaping school performance: A critical literature review.* Chicago, IL: University of Chicago Consortium on Chicago School Research.

Ferguson, R. F., Phillips, S. F., Rowley, J. F. S., & Friedlander, J. W. (2015). *The influence of teaching beyond standardized test scores: Engagement, mindsets, and agency.* Seattle, WA: Raikes Foundation.

Fisher, D., Frey, N., Quaglia, R., Smith, D., & Lande, L. (2018). *Engagement by design.* Thousand Oaks, CA: Corwin.

Fosen, D. M. (2016). *Developing good teacher-student relationships: A multiple-case study of six teachers' relational strategies and perceptions of closeness to students.* London, England: Institute of Education, University College London.

Fox, J. (2014). *Your child's strengths.* New York, NY: Penguin Books.

Fox-Eades, J. (2008). *Celebrating strength.* Coventry, England: CAPP Press.

Fredricks, J., Blumenfeld, P., & Paris, A. (2004). School engagement: Potential of the concept, state of the evidence. *Review of Educational Research, 74(1)*, 59-110.

Fredriksen, K., & Rhodes, J. (2004). *The role of teacher relationships in the lives of students.* New Directions for Youth Development, 103, 45-54.

Fredrickson, B. L. (2001). The role of positive emotions in positive psychology: The broaden-and-build theory of positive emotions. *American Psychologist, 56*, 218-226.

Furrer, C. J., & Skinner, E. A. (2003). Sense of relatedness as a factor in children's academic engagement and performance. *Journal of Education Psychology, 95*, 148-162.

Furrer, C. J., & Skinner, E. A. (2009). *Reciprocal effects of student engagement in the classroom on changes in teacher support over the school year.* Poster presented at the biennial meeting of the Society for Research in Child Development, Denver, CO.

Furrer, C. J., Skinner, E. A., & Pitzer, J. R. (2014). The influence of teacher and peer relationships on students' classroom engagement and everyday motivational resilience. *National Society for the Study of Education, 113(1)*, 101-123.

Gehlbach, H., Brinkworth, M. E., & Harris, A. D. (2012). Changes in teacher-student relationships. *British Journal of Educational Psychology, 82(4)*, 690-704.

Gehlbach, H., Brinkworth, M. E., Hsu, L., King, A., McIntyre, J., & Rogers, T. (2015). Creating birds of similar feathers: Leveraging similarity to improve teacher-student relationships and academic achievement. *Journal of Educational Psychology, 108(3)*, 342-52.

Gielan, M. (2015). *Broadcasting happiness.* Dallas, TX: Benbella Books.

Goyal, N., & Alternative Education Resource Organization. (2012). *One size does not fit all: A student's assessment of school.* Roslyn Heights, NY: Alternative Education Resource Organization.

Gregory, A., & Weinstein, R. S. (2004). Connection and regulation at home and in school: Predicting growth in achievement for adolescents. *Journal of Adolescent Research, 19*, 405-427.

Hamre, B. K., & Pianta, R. C. (2001). Early teacher-child relationships and the trajectory of children's school outcomes through eighth grade. *Child Development, 72(2)*, 625-638.

Haskins, W. (2000). Ethos and pedagogical communication: Suggestions for enhancing credibility in the classroom. *Current Issues in Education, 3(4).*

Hattie, J. (2009). *Visible learning: A synthesis of over 800 meta-analyses relating to achievement.* Oxford, England: Routledge.

Hattie, J. (2012). *Visible learning for teachers: Maximizing impact on achievement.* Oxford, England: Routledge.

Hattie, J., & Anderman, E.M. (Eds.) (2013). *International guide to student achievement.* London, England/New York, NY: Routledge.

Hattie, J., & Yates, G. (2014). *Visible learning and the science of how we learn.* London, England: Routledge/Taylor & Francis.

Hattie, J., & Timperley, H. (2007). The power of feedback. *Review of Educational Research, 77(1)*, 81-112.

Hines, C., Cruickshank, D., & Kennedy, J. (1985). Teacher clarity and its relationship to student achievement and satisfaction. *American Educational Research Journal, 22(1)*, 87-99.

Hoerr, T. (2016). *Formative five.* Alexandria, VA: Association for Supervision and Curriculum Development.

Hughes, J. N. (2011). Longitudinal effects of teacher and student perceptions of teacher-student relationship qualities on academic adjustment. *Elementary School Journal, 112*, 38-60.

Hughes, J. N. (2012). Teacher-student relationships and school adjustment: Progress and remaining challenges. *Attachment and Human Development, 14*, 319-327.

Hughes, J. N. (2017). Trajectories of teacher-student warmth and conflict at the transition to middle school: Effects on academic engagement and achievement. *Journal of School Psychology, 67*, 148-62.

Hughes, J. N., Gleason, K. A., & Zhang, D. (2005). Relationship influences on teachers' perceptions of academic competence in academically at risk minority and majority first grade students. *Journal of School Psychology, 43*, 303-320.

Hughes, J. N., & Kwok, O. M. (2006). Classroom engagement mediates the effect of teacher-student support on elementary students' peer acceptance: A prospective analysis. *Journal of School Psychology, 43*, 465-480.

Hughes, J. N., Luo, W., Kwok, O. M., & Loyd, L. K. (2008). Teacher-student support, effortful engagement, and achievement: A 3-year longitudinal study. *Journal of Educational Psychology, 100*, 1-14.

Hulleman, C. S., & Harackiewicz, J. M. (2009). Making education relevant: Increasing interest and performance in high school science classes. *Science, 326*, 1410–1412.

Hulleman, C. S., Schrager, S. M., Bodmann, S. M., & Harackiewicz, J. M. (2010). A meta-analytic review of achievement goal measures: Different labels for the same constructs or different constructs with similar labels? *Psychological Bulletin, 136*, 422-449.

Igel, C., & Urquhart, V. (2012). Generation Z, meet cooperative learning. *Middle School Journal, 43(4)*, 16.

Iso-Ahola, S. E., & Dotson, C. O. (2016). Psychological momentum: A key to continued success. *Frontiers in Psychology, 7*, 1328.

Jensen, E. (2005). *Teaching with the brain in mind* (2nd ed.). Alexandria, VA: Association for Supervision and Curriculum Development.

Jerome, E. M., Hamre, B. K., & Pianta, R. C. (2008). Teacher-child relationships from kindergarten to sixth grade: Early childhood predictors of teacher-perceived conflict and closeness. *Social Development, 18*, 915-945.

Johnson, D. W., & Johnson, R. (1989). *Cooperation and competition: Theory and research.* Edina, MN: Interaction Book Company.

Johnson, D. W., & Johnson, R. T. (2006). Peace education for consensual peace: The essential role of conflict resolution. *Journal of Peace Education, 3(2)*, 147-174.

Jussim, L. (1989). Teacher expectations: Self-fulfilling prophecies, perceptual biases, and accuracy. *Journal of Personality and Social Psychology, 57*, 469-480.

Justice, L. M., Cottone, E. A., & Rimm-Kaufman, S. E. (2008). Relationships between teachers and preschoolers who are at risk: Contribution of children's language skills, temperamentally based attributes, and gender. *Early Education and Development, 19*, 600-621.

Kleinfeld, J. (1975). Effective teachers of Eskimo and Indian students. *School Review, 83(2)*, 301-344.

Klem, A. M., & Connell, J. P. (2004). Relationships matter: Linking teacher support to student engagement and achievement. *Journal of School Health, 74*, 262-273.

Kluger, A. N., & DeNisi, A. (1996). The effects of feedback interventions on performance: A historical review, a meta-analysis, and a preliminary feedback intervention theory. *Psychological Bulletin, 119(2)*, 254.

Koepke, M. F., & Harkins, D. A. (2008). Conflict in the classroom: Gender differences in the teacher-child relationship. *Early Education & Development, 19*, 843-864.

Ladd, G. W., & Burgess, K. B. (2001). Do relational risks and protective factors moderate the linkages between childhood aggression and early psychological and school adjustment? *Child Development, 72*, 1579-1601.

Ladson-Billings, G. (1994). *The dreamkeepers: Successful teachers of African-American children.* San Francisco, CA: Jossey-Bass

La Guardia, J. G., & Patrick, H. (2008). Self-determination theory as a fundamental theory of close relationships. *Canadian Psychology, 49*, 201-209.

Lee, J. S. (2011). The effects of the teacher-student relationship and academic press on student engagement and academic performance. *International Journal of Educational Research, 53*, 330-340.

Lee, J. S. (2014). The relationship between student engagement and academic performance: Is it a myth or reality? *Journal of Educational Research, 107(3)*, 177–185.

Lyubomirsky, S., Sheldon, K. M., & Schkade, D. (2005). Pursuing happiness: The architecture of sustainable change. *Review of General Psychology, 9*, 111-131.

Malecki, C. K., & Demaray, M. K. (2003). What type of support do they need? Investigating student adjustment as related to emotional, informational, appraisal, and instrumental support. *School Psychology Quarterly, 18*, 231-252.

Marks, H. M. (2000). Student engagement in instructional activity: Patterns in the elementary, middle, and high school years. *American Educational Research Journal, 37(1)*, 153-184.

Martin, A. J. (2006a). A motivational psychology for the education of Indigenous students. *Australian Journal of Indigenous Education, 35*, 30-43.

Martin, A. J. (2006b). *Pastoral pedagogy: A great composition comprising the song, the singer, and the singing.* Washington, DC: U.S. Department of Education.

Martin, A. J., & Dowson, M. (2009). Interpersonal relationships, motivation, engagement, and achievement: Yields for theory, current issues, and educational practice. *Review of Educational Research, 79*, 327-365.

Martin, A. J., & Marsh, H. W. (2006). Academic resilience and its psychological and educational correlates: A construct validity approach. P*sychology in the Schools, 43*, 267-282.

Martin, A. J., Marsh, H. W., McInerney, D. M., Green, J., & Dowson, M. (2007). Getting along with teachers and parents: The yields of good relationships for students' achievement motivation and self-esteem. *Australian Journal of Guidance and Counselling, 17*, 109-125.

Mashburn, A. J., Pianta, R. C., Hamre, B. K., Downer, J. T., Barbarin, O. A., Bryant, D., & Howes, C. (2008). Measures of classroom quality in prekindergarten and children's development of academic, language, and social skills. *Child Development, 79*, 732-749.

McCaleb, J., & Rosenthal, B. (1983). Relationships in teacher clarity between students' perceptions and observers' ratings. *Journal of Classroom Interaction, 19(1)*, 15-21.

McCaleb, J., & White, J. (1980). Critical dimensions in evaluating teacher clarity. *Journal of Classroom Interaction, 15(2)*, 27-30.

McCroskey, J. C., Valencic, K. M., & Richmond, V. P. (2004). Toward a general model of instructional communication. *Communication Quarterly, 52*, 197-210.

McGrath, K. F., & Van Bergen, P. (2015). Who, when, why, and to what end? Students at risk of negative student-teacher relationships and their outcomes. *Educational Research Review, 14*, 1-17.

McKown, C., & Weinstein, R. S. (2008). Teacher expectations, classroom context, and the achievement gap. *Journal of School Psychology, 46*, 235-261.

Medcalf, J. (2015). *Chop wood, carry water: How to fall in love with the process of becoming great.* Scotts Valley, CA: CreateSpace Independent Publishing Platform.

Meehan, B. T., Hughes, J. N., & Cavell, T. A. (2003). Teacher-student relationships as compensatory resources for aggressive children. *Child Development, 74*, 1145-1157.

Meissel, K., Meyer, F., Yao, E. S., & Rubie-Davies, C. M. (2017). Subjectivity of teacher judgment: Exploring student characteristics that influence teacher judgments of student ability. *Teaching and Teacher Education, 65*, 48-60.

Middleton, M., & Perks, K. (2014). *Motivation to learn.* Boston, MA: Corwin.

Milatz, A., Lüftenegger, M., & Schober, B. (2015). Teachers' relationship closeness with students as a resource for teacher wellbeing: A response surface analytical approach. *Frontier in Psychology, 6*, 1-16.

Morganett, L. (2001). Good teacher-student relationships: A key element in classroom motivation and management. *Education, 112(2)*, 260-265.

Murdock, T. B., Anderman, L. H., & Hodge, S. A. (2000). Middle-grade predictors of students' motivation and behavior in high school. *Journal of Adolescent Research, 15(3)*, 327-351.

Murray, C. (2009). Parent and teacher relationships as predictors of school engagement and functioning among low-income urban youth. *Journal of Early Adolescence, 29*, 376-404.

Nathan, M., & Petrosino, A. (2003). Expert blind spot among preservice teachers. *American Educational Research Journal, 40(4)*, 905-928.

National Scientific Council on the Developing Child. (2015). *Supportive relationships and active skill-building strengthen the foundations of resilience* (Working Paper 13). Retrieved from http://www.developingchild.harvard.edu

Nelson, R. M., & DeBacker, T. K. (2008). Achievement motivation in adolescents: The role of peer climate and best friends. *Journal of Experimental Education, 76*, 170-189.

Newberry, M. (2013). Reconsidering differential behaviors: Reflection and teacher judgment when forming classroom relationships. *Teacher Development, 17(2)*, 195-213.

Niemiec, C. P., & Ryan, R. M. (2009). Autonomy, competence, and relatedness in the classroom: Applying self-determination theory to educational practice. *Theory and Research in Education, 7*, 133-144.

Nottingham, J. (2017). *The learning challenge: How to guide your students through the learning pit to achieve deeper understanding.* Thousand Oaks, CA: Corwin.

Pajares, F., & Urdan, T. (Eds.). (2006). Adolescence and education: Vol. 5. *Self-efficacy beliefs of adolescents.* Greenwich, CT: Information Age.

Palmer, P. (1998). *The courage to teach: Exploring the inner landscape of a teacher's life.* San Francisco, CA: Jossey-Bass.

Pepler, D. J., & Bierman, K. L. (2018). *With a little help from my friends: The importance of peer relationships for social-emotional development.* State College, PA: Edna Bennett Pierce Prevention Research Center, Pennsylvania State University.

Perrell, A., Erdie, J., & Kasay, T. (2019). *What motivates students to learn? Applications for all classroom levels.* Retrieved from https://journals.uncc.edu/jaepr/article/view/658/633

Pianta, R. C. (1999). *Enhancing relationships between children and teachers.* Washington, DC: American Psychological Association.

Pianta, R. C., & Allen, J. P. (2008). Building capacity for positive youth development in secondary school classroom: Changing teachers' interactions with students. In M. Shinn & H. Yoshikawa (Eds.), *Toward positive youth development: Transforming schools and community programs* (pp. 21-39). Oxford, England: Oxford University Press.

Pianta, R. C., Belsky, J., Vandergrift, N., Houts, R., & Morrison, F. J. (2008). Classroom effects on children's achievement trajectories in elementary school. *American Educational Research Journal, 45*, 365-397.

Pianta, R. C., Hamre, B. K., & Allen, J. P. (2012). Teacher-student relationships and engagement: Conceptualizing, measuring, and improving the capacity of classroom interactions. In S. L. Christenson, A. L. Reschly, & C. Wylie (Eds.), *Handbook of research on student engagement* (pp. 365-386). New York, NY: Springer.

Pianta, R. C., Hamre, B., & Stuhlman, M. (2003). Relationships between teachers and children. In W. M. Reynolds, G. E. Miller, & I. B. Weiner (Eds.), *Handbook of psychology: Educational psychology* (Vol. 7, pp. 199-234). Hoboken, NJ: John Wiley.

Pianta, R. C., & Nimetz, S. L. (1991). Relationships between children and teachers: Associations with classroom and home behavior. *Journal of Applied Developmental Psychology, 12*, 379-393.

Pianta, R. C., Nimetz, S. L., & Bennet, E. (1997). Mother-child relationships, teacher-child relationships, and school outcomes in preschool and kindergarten. *Early Childhood Research Quarterly, 12*, 263-280.

Pianta, R. C., & Stuhlman, M. W. (2004). Teacher-child relationships and children's success in the first years of school. *School Psychology Review, 33*, 444-458.

Pink, D. (2011). *Drive.* New York, NY: Penguin Group.

Pratt, S., & George, R. (2005). Transferring friendship: Girls' and boys' friendships in the transition from primary to secondary school. *Children & Society, 19*, 16-26.

Rabinovitz, J. (2013). *Nobel laureate appointed Stanford professor of education.* Retrieved from https://ed.stanford.edu/news/nobel-laureate-appointedstanford-professor-physics-and-education

Reeve, J. (2009). Why teachers adopt a controlling motivating style toward students and how they can become more autonomy supportive. *Educational Psychologist, 44*, 159-175.

Reeve, J., Deci, E. L., & Ryan, R. M. (2004). Self-determination theory: A dialectical framework for understanding the sociocultural influences on student motivation. In D. McInerney & S. Van Etten (Eds.), *Research on sociocultural influences on motivation and learning: Big theories revisited* (Vol. 4, pp. 31–59). Greenwich, CT: Information Age.

Reeve, J., & Halusic, M. (2009). How K–12 teachers can put self-determination theory principles into practice. *Theory and Research in Education, 7*, 145-154.

Reeve, J., & Jang, H. (2006). What teachers say and do to support students' autonomy during a learning activity. *Journal of Educational Psychology, 98*, 209-218.

Reeve, J., & Tseng, C.-M. (2011). Agency as a fourth aspect of students' engagement during learning activities. *Contemporary Educational Psychology, 36*, 257-267.

Rimm-Kaufman, S. (2011). *Improving students' relationships with teachers to provide essential supports for learning.* Retrieved from http://www.apa.org/education/k12/relationships.aspx

Rogers, C. R. (1969). *Freedom to learn.* Columbus, OH: Charles E. Merrill.

Roorda, D. L., Koomen, M. Y., Spilt, J. L., Oort, F. L. (2011). The influence of affective teacher-student relationships on students' school engagement and achievement: A meta-analytic approach. *Review of Educational Research, 81*, 493-529.

Rosenthal, R., & Jacobson, L. (1968). *Pygmalion in the classroom: Teacher expectation and students' intellectual development.* New York, NY: Holt, Rinehart and Winston.

Rubie-Davies, C. M. (2017). *Teacher expectations in education.* Oxford, England: Routledge.

Rubie-Davies, C. M. (2007). Classroom interactions: Exploring the practices of high-and low-expectation teachers. *British Journal of Educational Psychology, 77(2)*, 289-306.

Rubie-Davies, C. M., Hattie, J., & Hamilton, R. (2006). Expecting the best for students: Teacher expectations and academic outcomes. *British Journal of Educational Psychology, 76(3)*, 429-444.

Rubie-Davies, C. M., & Peterson, E. (2011). Teacher expectations and beliefs: Their influence onthe socioemotional environment in the classroom. In C. M. Rubie-Davies (Ed.), *Educational psychology concepts, research and challenges* (pp. 134-149). London, England: Routledge.

Ruzek, E. A., Hafen, C. A., Allen, J. P., Gregory, A., Mikami, A. Y., & Pianta, R. C. (2016). How teacher emotional support motivates students: The mediating roles of perceived peer relatedness, autonomy support, and competence. *Learning and Instruction, 42*, 95-103.

Ryan, R. M., & Deci, E. L. (2000). Self-determination theory and the facilitation of intrinsic motivation, social development, and well-being. *American Psychologist, 55*, 68-78.

Ryan, R. M., & Deci, E. L. (2002). Overview of self-determination theory: An organismic dialectical perspective. In E. L. Deci & R. M. Ryan (Eds.), *Handbook of self-determination theory research* (pp. 3-33). Rochester, NY: Rochester University Press.

Ryan, R. M., Stiller, J., & Lynch, J. H. (1994). Representations of relationships to parents, teachers, and friends as predictors of academic motivation and self-esteem. *Journal of Early Adolescence, 14*, 226-249.

Sabol, T., & Pianta, R. C. (2012). Recent trends in research on teacher-child relationships. *Attachment and Human Development, 14.*

Schunk, D. H. (1991). Self-efficacy and academic motivation. *Educational Psychologist, 26*, 207-31.

Skinner, E. A., & Pitzer, J. R. (2012). Developmental dynamics of engagement, coping, and everyday resilience. In S. Christenson, A. Reschly, & C. Wylie (Eds.), *Handbook of research on student engagement* (pp. 21-44). New York, NY: Springer Science.

Skipper, Y., & Douglas, K. (2012). Is no praise good praise? Effects of positive feedback on children's and university students' responses to subsequent failures. *British Journal of Educational Psychology, 82(2)*, 327-39.

Skipper, Y., & Douglas, K. (2015). The influence of teacher feedback on children's perceptions of student-teacher relationships. *British Journal of Educational Psychology, 85*, 276-288.

Spilt, J. L., & Koomen, H. M. Y. (2009). Widening the view on teacher-child relationships: Teachers' narratives concerning disruptive versus non-disruptive children. *School Psychology Review, 38*, 86-101.

Spilt, J. L., Koomen, H. M. Y., & Thijs, J. T. (2011). Teacher wellbeing: The importance of student-teacher relationships. *Educational Psychology Review, 23*, 457-477.

Sugarman, J. (2017). The rise of teen depression. *Johns Hopkins Health Review, 4(2)*, 42-51.

Teven, J. J., & McCroskey, J. C. (1997). The relationship of perceived teacher caring with student learning and teacher evaluation. *Communication Education, 46*, 1-9.

The New Teacher Project (TTNP). (2018). *The opportunity myth.* Brooklyn, NY: Author.

Valiente, C., Lemery-Chalfant, K., Swanson, J., & Reiser, M. (2008). Prediction of children's academic competence from their effortful control, relationships, and classroom participation. *Journal of Educational Psychology, 100*, 67-77.

Vansteenkiste, M., Lens, M., & Deci, E. L. (2006). Intrinsic versus extrinsic goal contents in self-determination theory: Another look at the quality of academic motivation. *Educational Psychologist, 41*, 19-31.

Vansteenkiste, M., Sierens, E., Soenens, B., Luyckx, K., & Lens, W. (2009). Motivational profiles from a self-determination perspective: The quality of motivation matters. *Journal of Educational Psychology, 101*, 671-688.

Visser, C. L. F., Ket, J. C., Croiset, G., & Kusurkar, R. A. (2017). Perceptions of residents, medical and nursing students about interprofessional education: A systematic review of the quantitative and qualitative literature. *BMC Medical Education, 17*, 77.

Vygotsky, L. S. (1978). *Mind in society: The development of higher psychological processes.* Cambridge, MA: Harvard University Press.

Wang, M. T., & Holcombe, R. (2010). Adolescents' perceptions of school environment, engagement, and academic achievement in middle school. *American Educational Research Journal, 47(3)*, 633-622.

Waters, L. (2017). *The strength switch: How the new science of strength-based parenting can help your child and your teen to flourish.* New York, NY: Penguin Group.

Weinstein, R. S., & McKown, C. (1998). Expectancy effects in context: Listening to the voices of students and teachers. In J. Brophy (Ed.), *Advances in research on teaching* (Vol. 7, pp. 215–242). Greenwich, CT: JAI Press.

Wellborn, J. G. (1991). *Engaged and disaffected action: The conceptualization and measurement of motivation in the academic domain* (Unpublished doctoral dissertation, University of Rochester).

Wentzel, K. R. (1997). Student motivation in middle school: The role of perceived pedagogical caring. *Journal of Educational Psychology, 89*, 411-419.

Wentzel, K. R. (1998). Social relationships and motivation in middle school: The role of parents, teachers, and peers. *Journal of Educational Psychology, 90,* 202-209.

Wentzel, K. R. (1999). Social-motivational processes and interpersonal relationships: Implications for understanding motivation at school. *Journal of Educational Psychology, 91*, 76-97.

Wentzel, K. R., McNamara Barry, C., & Caldwell, K. A. (2004). Friendships in middle school: Influences on motivation and school adjustment. *Journal of Educational Psychology, 96*, 195-203.

Wentzel, K. R. (2009a). Students' relationships with teachers as motivational contexts. In K. Wentzel & A. Wigfield (Eds.), *Handbook of motivation in school* (pp. 301-322). Mahwah, NJ: Erlbaum.

Wentzel, K. R. (2009b). Peers and academic functioning at school. In K. H. Rubin, W. M. Bukowski, & B. Laursen (Eds.). *Handbook of peer interactions, relationships and groups* (pp. 531-547). New York, NY: Guilford Press.

Wentzel, K. R. (2012). *Teacher-student relationships and adolescent competence at school interpersonal relationships in education* (pp. 19–35). New York, NY: Springer.

Wentzel, K. (2013). *Motivating students to learn.* London, England: Routledge.

Williams, E. (1985). *Research on teacher clarity.* Teacher Education Quarterly, 12(3), 33-38.

Wubbels, T., & Brekelmans, M. (2005). Two decades of research on teacher-student relationships in class. *International Journal of Educational Research, 43*, 6-24.

Yeager, D. S., Purdie-Vaughns, V., Garcia, J., Apfel, N., Brzustoski, P., Master, A., Cohen, G. L. (2014). Breaking the cycle of mistrust: Wise interventions to provide critical feedback across the racial divide. *Journal of Experimental Psychology: General, 143(2)*, 804-24.

Youniss, J., & Haynie, D. L. (1992). Friendship in adolescence. *Developmental and Behavioral Pediatrics, 13*, 59-66.

Zhang, Y. (2014). Educational expectations, school experiences and academic achievements: A longitudinal examination. *China: An International Journal, 12*, 43-65.

Zierer, K., & Hattie, J. (2017). *10 mindframes for visible learning: Teaching for success.* Oxford, England: Routledge.

Zimmerman, B. J. (2000). Self-efficacy: An essential motive to learn. *Contemporary Educational Psychology, 25*, 82–91.

ABOUT FIRST

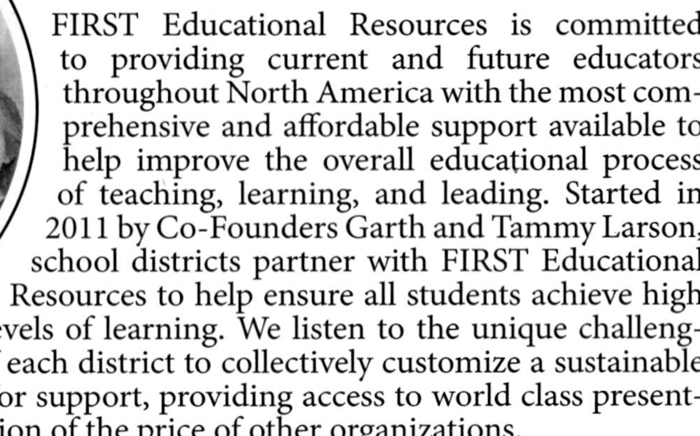

FIRST Educational Resources is committed to providing current and future educators throughout North America with the most comprehensive and affordable support available to help improve the overall educational process of teaching, learning, and leading. Started in 2011 by Co-Founders Garth and Tammy Larson, school districts partner with FIRST Educational Resources to help ensure all students achieve high levels of learning. We listen to the unique challenges of each district to collectively customize a sustainable solution for support, providing access to world class presenters at a fraction of the price of other organizations.

Using our Learning FIRST Framework (below), FIRST Educational Resources offers a variety of services to help support this mission, including our Learning FIRST Institutes, professional workshops and conferences, consulting and coaching services, on-site solutions, publications, graduate level programs, and assisting districts with administrator searches.

Educational Topics WE Support Throughout North America Include:

- Assessment and Grading
- Collaboration
- Culture
- Equity
- Innovation
- Instruction
- Leadership
- Professional Learning Communities
- Relationships in Schools
- Response to Intervention/MTSS
- Social Emotional Learning

For more information on becoming a partnership district with **FIRST Educational Resources**, please contact us at ***(920) 479-6504*** or email us at **info@firsteducation-us.com** and we would be happy to assist in your professional learning needs. We guarantee we can save you money in your professional learning, while giving you an unsurpassed experience in moving the professional learning forward in your district the right way. We look forward to working with you!